The Adaptable Degree

This book utilized a mixed-methods research study of the career experiences of theatre graduates in the U.S. to provide data on employment patterns and job satisfaction. With a population of over 1,000 participants, this study examined where graduates were working, how their careers had changed over time, which skills acquired with their theatre degree were being used in current employment, and whether they believed their course of study was worth the financial investment, given their current circumstances. Evidence from this study revealed that a theatre degree provided many of the skills the employment market is currently seeking and that theatre graduates were gainfully employed in multiple sectors of the economy. This important data-based, field-specific information will aid chairs, deans, provosts, politicians, students and parents in decision-making at a time when arts and humanities departments across the country are under the threat of elimination.

Melanie Dreyer-Lude is an American theatre artist/scholar specializing in international theatre collaboration and multidisciplinary projects. She is a professor in the Department of Drama at the University of Alberta and lives and works in Edmonton, Alberta, Canada.

Routledge Advances in Theatre & Performance Studies

This series is our home for cutting-edge, upper-level scholarly studies and edited collections. Considering theatre and performance alongside topics such as religion, politics, gender, race, ecology, and the avant-garde, titles are characterized by dynamic interventions into established subjects and innovative studies on emerging topics.

Teaching Dance Improvisation
A Beginner's Guide
Matthew Farmer

1000 Ways to Ask Why
Introduction to Dramaturgical Thinking
Emily LeQuesne

Making a Scene
Creating a Scene Study Class for Actors
Bill Gelber

Music and Sound in European Theatre
Practices, Performances, Perspectives
Edited by David Roesner and Tamara Yasmin Quick

The Adaptable Degree
How Education in Theatre Supports the Economy of the Future
Melanie Dreyer-Lude

For more information about this series, please visit: www.routledge.com/Routledge-Advances-in-Theatre--Performance-Studies/book-series/RATPS

The Adaptable Degree

How Education in Theatre Supports the Economy of The Future

Melanie Dreyer-Lude

LONDON AND NEW YORK

First published 2025
by Routledge
4 Park Square, Milton Park, Abingdon, Oxon OX14 4RN

and by Routledge
605 Third Avenue, New York, NY 10158

Routledge is an imprint of the Taylor & Francis Group, an informa business

British Library Cataloguing-in-Publication Data
A catalogue record for this book is available from the British Library

ISBN: 9781032858265 (hbk)
ISBN: 9781032858333 (pbk)
ISBN: 9781003520023 (ebk)

DOI: 10.4324/9781003520023

Typeset in Times New Roman
by codeMantra

For every student I have had the privilege to teach, the parents who want to support their dreams, and the colleagues who share my passion for theatre.

Contents

Acknowledgments

First thanks goes to Lofty Durham whose editing prowess was instrumental in shaping this book. He has been and continues to be an indispensable writing mentor. Thanks to Sarah Thornton, my grad school colleague, for encouraging me to pursue this study. Without that nudge, I'm not sure I would have had the courage. Thanks to Dr. Cynthia MacGregor, my dissertation supervisor, who shepherded the journey of this theatre specialist through graduate study in the field of education. She was a brilliant guide who was generous with her advice and demanded rigor in all of my work. Thanks to my dissertation committee who encouraged me to publish the findings in my doctoral study: Dr. Kennedy Ongaga (an incredibly kind man), Dr. Marissa Weaver (who continues to inspire me), and Dr. A. Leslie Anderson (who bravely joined our committee with no knowledge of the content that she would encounter). I also want to acknowledge the following colleagues who have helped shape my thoughts on this subject: Dr. Itai Cohen, Dr. Lynne Conner, Dr. Piet Defraeye, Dr. Attilio Favorini, Seana Manning Hale, Dr. Christopher Herr, Michael Kaplan, David Kennedy, Doug Mertz, Dr. Stefano Muneroni, Dr. Michael O'Driscoll, Dr. Jennifer Pierce, and Susi Varvayanis.

Introduction

Theatre transformed me, although I did not discover the joy of live storytelling until I was 14 years old. I was painfully shy, the victim of upper-class bullying, and just trying to get through the nightmare of middle school. It was my best friend, Jodean Smith, who encouraged me to audition for the school play. This seemed a ridiculous idea at the time as I believed I could better improve my popularity quotient by joining the cheerleading squad not by becoming a drama geek. But I did not do well at the cheerleading try-out as my voice was small and no one could hear me. Reluctantly, I agreed to give the drama thing a try. I was cast in that first play only because an incredible teacher named Don Faulkner saw something in me that others had not. By opening night, after overcoming my fear of public performance and tripling the size of my very small voice, I knew I had found my home. Within only a few months, my social confidence increased, and by the time I reached high school, I had become one of the popular kids.

Although I sometimes wonder what my life would have been like if I had chosen to pursue that marine biology dream, a career in the theatre has worked well for me. It has not been easy. My path has included numerous side roads, major obstacles, crushing defeats, and financial struggles. I regret nothing. Over the past several decades, I have directed almost 80 live theatre productions, performed in a couple of dozen plays, started two theatre companies, traveled to almost every continent, and had the privilege of sharing my passion for storytelling with thousands of college students. Not a bad career, all in all. But this discipline that I love, the course of study that transformed me from an awkward, shy adolescent to a confident and ambitious adult human is beginning to disappear on college campuses. Between 2017 and 2024, at least 18 theatre programs had been cut or absorbed into other disciplines. Politicians and the general public appear convinced that arts study is optional, and in times of fiscal crisis, the optional is the first to go. Those faced with balancing budgets must answer to a public that is understandably outraged at the cost of a college education while simultaneously recognizing that advanced learning is an important ticket to gainful employment. Arts educators who have been passionately advocating for their courses of study have struggled

DOI: 10.4324/9781003520023-1

to provide arguments that persuasively demonstrate the employment value of an arts degree. They recognize the extraordinary skills they impart to their students, but communicating the positive employment impact of those skills has been a challenge.

Over a decade ago, I began to have ethical misgivings about teaching acting and directing to young aspiring artists, given the grim state of our field. I struggled with the reality that I might be educating my students for inevitable unemployment. I have managed to stay in touch with many of my former students and to witness the journeys their career paths have taken. Some have become lawyers, doctors, arts consultants, or forest rangers. A few of them have enjoyed bumpy yet successful careers in the entertainment industry. When considering these individual narratives, I recognized that many of these theatre graduates had found employment and were thriving, each following their own independent and unique career trajectory. Could it be that a theatre degree does make one employable? Perhaps in multiple fields? These were the questions that drove me to engage in this study. I wanted to know what to tell students about potential future employment and whether their investment of tens of thousands of dollars would provide a reliable return. My study revealed some important information for aspiring theatre students and the educators who train them. Not only is theatre study not "optional" in today's job market, but the skills theatre students acquire have become some of those most highly sought by employers. We now live in a world in which abilities like interpersonal communication, adaptive problem-solving, and creativity are at a premium. This presents an opportunity to change the message.

Employers are hungry for applicants with a wide array of transferable skills, and many of those skills are a core component of a theatre degree. Opportunities to learn these skills are often unavailable in other courses of study suggesting that some theatre education could contribute to the employability of every college student. The need for transferable skills for employment in today's job market means that removing arts programs like theatre may end up undermining an institution's ability to make students more employable. A theatre degree is unlikely to turn the average college graduate into a full-time theatre artist, but a theatre major, minor, or just a class or two can enhance employability in an astonishing array of fields. College graduates require skills that can adapt to a dynamic job market as 40% of them will end up working in a field different from their chosen major.[1] Labor statistics indicate that the average college graduate will change jobs 12 times over the course of their career.[2] Studying theatre is an asset in this dynamic environment and we need to telegraph this message to university administrators, those seeking a college degree, and the general public.

Although many theatre educators are aware of the value of a theatre degree, it can be challenging to deliver this message in a way that has an impact on curricula, programs, and budgets. General arguments about the value of the arts in a well-rounded education struggle to hold sway. Those in charge of distributing precious financial resources are looking at numbers that telegraph that theatre programs are expensive and job prospects for graduates are grim. As state governments continue to reduce funding for higher education and tuition continues to climb, it can be hard to justify a theatre program when there are so few jobs available in the field.[3] Theatre departments emerged in higher education in response to a growing theatre industry and adapted their curriculum to prepare stage-ready professionals. For over a century, theatre educators have provided training for artists intending to work in the field of theatre, but that field and the economy that supports it have now shifted. To survive, theatre departments need to adapt to the reality that confronts them. Only a fraction of theatre graduates will end up with life-long careers as working theatre artists. There are not enough jobs in the theatre to accommodate every graduate, but the training every theatre student receives is of value to a dynamic job market that includes and transcends traditional theatre work.

To shift the perception of the value of a theatre degree, theatre educators and the administrators who support them need to change the message. This book offers evidence that theatre graduates not only find work but that work may be well-remunerated in a wide variety of fields. This evidence can support an argument for retaining and possibly increasing the scope and availability of theatre training on a college campus. Theatre educators can combat threats to their programs through a variety of strategies. They can develop workshops, classes, or project-based learning initiatives designed to share the transferable skills they teach with students in other disciplines. They can engage their alumni, particularly those alumni who have shifted careers, and invite them to talk with theatre students about multiple possible career pathways. They can actively partner with their deans in advocating for their programs by providing evidence of the multidisciplinary value of the training they provide. And finally, theatre educators can help theatre students recognize the transferable skills they are learning and the application of those skills to a variety of paradigms. A more conscious explication of these skills during theatre training might provide opportunities for students to see how to apply these ideas outside of a theatre context. Should a theatre graduate choose to shift fields or work simultaneously in another field, understanding how to identify these abilities to a current or prospective employer could create a professional advantage. Recognizing the interdisciplinary value of a theatre degree may also help mitigate feelings of shame or failure for those who choose to leave the theatre. Associating these skills with positive attributes creates room for graduates to see their educational background as an advantage rather than a mistake. Indeed, framing multiple future employment prospects for theatre graduates may help ease the anxiety of the transition into the professional marketplace and present more inter- or cross-disciplinary possibilities for all graduates. Whatever the tactic, the time to act is now. What theatre programs have to offer is of value to every student on campus. It is up to us to protect those educational opportunities.

Notes

1 Humphreys, D., & Kelly, P. (2014). How liberal arts and sciences majors fare in employment: A report on earnings and long-term career paths. *Peer Review, 16*(2), 31–32.
2 Gallup (Firm). (2019). Forging pathways to purposeful work: The role of higher education. Bates College.
3 Selingo, J. J. (2013). *College (un) bound: The future of higher education and what it means for students*. Houghton Mifflin Harcourt.

1 Passion versus practicality

A high school student and her parents sit in my office ready to talk about majoring in theatre. This prospective student is bright-eyed, excited, and ready to enroll. Her mother wants to be supportive, but she needs more information on course content, the size of the classes, the average time to graduation, and employment prospects once her child has the degree. Her father says little and looks bleak. I have had this meeting many times, watching parents balance the wish to make their child happy against the real cost of a college degree and the prospects it may or may not bring. Often, hopeful theatre students were key players in high school theatre programs. There, in situations built on collaboration, overcoming constant obstacles, and finally achieving the success of an opening night, students may experience the heady feeling of belonging and accomplishment for the first time. Sometimes they are encouraged by mentors to pursue a career in the theatre. Perhaps they just wish to duplicate the joy and the fun they experienced while putting on a show. With or without talent, clear-eyed about what they want or just making the easiest choice, these students enter a college program with hopes and dreams. Anyone funding a college degree brings expectations to this new institutional relationship whether student or parent. They recognize that a college degree is important, but that they could end up spending tens of thousands of dollars on a course of study that might do little for future employment.

Do I need a college degree?

Research has demonstrated that, although a college degree is not required for all positions, those who hold at least some study at the undergraduate level will earn more money over their lifetimes than those with only a high school diploma.[1] High school graduates seeking university study may find that tuition costs have become prohibitive or, at the very least, influence where and what they study. The cost of college has tripled since the 1970s, a burden that has brought into question whether a college degree is worth the price.[2] In the current economic climate, the question driving college selection seems to be "How much will I earn if I major in this field at this institution versus that

DOI: 10.4324/9781003520023-2

one?" Labor statistics can help identify which majors lead to higher salaries, and well-situated employment upon graduation can serve as the determining factor when deciding where to study and what to choose as a major.[3] For those who may be footing the bill for tuition and room and board, these factors are important. Although they may appreciate the character-building value of higher education, they need to understand what their money will buy and how this investment will contribute to their future. As one parent put it during a freshman orientation event in Andrew Rossi's documentary *Ivory Tower*, "What you're saying is all very nice, but we're about to lay out a whole lot of money to you. Tell me one thing, is my daughter going to have a job when she graduates?"[4]

The reality of being an arts grad

When they graduate, arts graduates of all disciplines enter a precarious employment environment in which they will often be underemployed and/or working in several jobs at once. Some may even choose to work for lower wages to retain logistical flexibility, allowing them to pivot to arts-related opportunities when they become available.[5] Researchers have argued that 90% of performance arts graduates will find themselves unemployed at some point in their careers and may never work professionally in their field of study. This creates an ethical conundrum for educators who are training students for jobs they may never experience.[6] Others have argued that unemployment figures for all liberal arts grads (of which theatre is a part) are exaggerated and that unemployment for this sector, at 3.6%, is only slightly higher than for STEM fields (science, technology, engineering, and math) at 3.4%.[7] According to the most recent SNAAP Aggregate Report (Strategic National Arts Alumni Project), 10% of arts graduates were unemployed and 19% had never been employed professionally as an artist, bringing into question the sensibility of choosing to pursue a career in the arts.[8]

What is becoming increasingly clear is the importance of the arts and creative industries in our current and emerging global economy. As technology and artificial intelligence increase in prominence, jobs that cannot be done by machines have more value. Skills that are core to arts education – creative problem-solving, adaptability, interpersonal communication – are critical in an economic marketplace that continues to change and evolve at a rapid pace. Innovation is essential to remain competitive, and arts and humanities degrees provide a framework that nurtures and develops innovative thinking.[9] A report by the National Endowment for the Arts identified that "The arts added four times more to the U.S. economy than the agricultural sector and $200 billion more than transportation or warehousing."[10] The fastest-growing areas in arts employment are web services and digital publishing. This was evident in a U.S. Labor Statistics report which projected an employment increase for entertainers of 6% from 2022 to 2032[11] with a predicted increase of 7% for producers and directors.[12] The employment prospects for theatre majors are complicated and evolving, but unemployment and poverty are not a foregone conclusion.

What employers want

In 2005, Daniel Pink predicted that creative thinkers and those with exceptional interpersonal skills would become more valuable to employers than those who had focused solely on core subjects like business, math, or science.[13] Using the argument of supply and demand, he claimed that the MFA had become the new MBA, a disruptive idea that quickly gained traction. According to Pink, employers had access to a glut of business graduates who had opted to acquire an MBA because they saw this degree as the key to prosperous and stable job placement. This influx of business graduates oversaturated the marketplace and depressed employment prospects for new MBA grads. To further complicate the picture, employers had discovered that what they really needed was not more business graduates but more creative types.[14] What originated as a rational and sensible educational decision (getting an MBA to improve earning potential) became for some a costly degree that failed to provide the skills the job market was seeking.

The decision to pursue an MBA during the 2000s made economic sense as growing concerns over rising student debt pressured students to graduate with a marketable degree within the shortest time possible.[15] For those choosing careers in sensible subjects like business or engineering, that meant narrowing their focus to only those classes required for graduation. This narrow band of study, however well intended, prepared them for some aspects of work in their field but left them wanting in others. They were fully equipped to map a business plan or design a bridge but could not effectively pitch ideas, creatively solve problems, or work well with a team of colleagues.[16] Jeff Selingo suggested that employers were more interested in skills than degrees. He identified that employers and prospective employees often have divergent views regarding how prepared applicants are to engage in employment with their company.[17] While employers seek applicants with imagination, creativity, teamwork, adaptability, and innovation so that their companies can remain competitive, applicants often lack these more intangible skills. These skills happen to be a core component of the pedagogy in a theatre degree and are present in many arts-based degrees. Rehearsing and presenting a play, an important part of the embodied learning activities in a theatre degree, requires students to develop skills in teamwork, interpersonal communication, conflict resolution, problem-solving, improvisation, public speaking, and leadership, to name only a few. These important abilities are not traditionally presented as targeted learning outcomes for those participating in theatre training. Rather, developing them is a natural byproduct of the study of theatre.[18] Arts education in all disciplines can begin building these skills at a young age. Sadly, cash-strapped school districts are eliminating the arts from their curriculum and money-minded college students often opt to take only those courses that will contribute directly to their non-arts degree.

Given that we cannot imagine what the job market will look like even five years in the future, it is important for college graduates to obtain flexible, adaptable skills that can be applied in several employment paradigms. Arts training can prepare students to succeed in a marketplace that requires this kind of adaptability.[19] As change in the job market continues to accelerate, those graduates who have acquired an adaptable skill set have the greatest chance of succeeding and thriving.[20] This is not to suggest that a degree in the arts is for everyone, but some of the training in arts study may benefit every degree. The tension between a Return on Investment for a college degree and this intangible skills gap appears to put prospective students in a bind.[21] If they have determined that a college degree is a ticket to future employment, which path should they choose to ensure success so that they may graduate with the least amount of debt and the greatest possibility of finding a job?

Passion can lead to prosperity

A degree in the arts provides many of the intangible skills employers seek. What it cannot guarantee is stable, lucrative employment in the field of study. But no college degree can make that promise. Even students in fields like law and medicine, courses of study that seem to offer optimistic job prospects, may find themselves struggling to find employment upon graduation. Many arts grads recognize that they are embarking on a career that will offer a collection of challenges, only some of them monetary. If they know they cannot make much money as an artist, why would they pursue this path? For some, money is one in a series of acceptable trade-offs. They may turn down the offer of a job with a great salary but no flexibility so that they are free to do work that brings them pleasure.[22] They may prefer the opportunity to practice their craft over the remuneration some forms of employment can provide.[23] It is not uncommon for recent graduates to cobble together a collection of arts-adjacent jobs that serve to support the process of building an arts career.[24]

These trade-offs and compromises might seem troubling; yet, many arts graduates indicate high satisfaction with their career choices even while wishing they had more opportunities to work professionally in their field.[25] The SNAAP Project has found that most arts graduates were happy with their education even though their choices may have resulted in periods of un- or underemployment.[26] What appeared most important to these graduates was the creative value of their career.[27] Daniel Pink wrote that right-brain thinkers, which he identified as artistic or creative types, were best positioned for professional happiness and opportunity in the job market of the future.[28]

Professional happiness and career satisfaction are central to recent curricular innovations in higher education, innovations like the Bates College Purposeful Work Program. At Bates, educators work carefully with students to align their interests and their skill sets and to help them choose a future career that will provide meaning. This process is designed to address the "purpose gap" for young graduates as they prepare to enter the job market.[29] It turns out that personal growth, achieving goals, and social interaction all contribute to the Return on Investment of a college education.[30] For some arts graduates, their education and career choices come from a calling, a sense of identity that when matched with a course of study may contribute to more positive employment outcomes.[31] High career satisfaction can lead to high life satisfaction,[32] while we must also recognize that career happiness may be influenced by an array of factors.[33]

What the survey told us

Theatre alumni who graduated from 1960 through 2020 offered a complex picture of employment pathways, motivations for selecting the degree, and a variety of perspectives on the results of their education in light of their current employment. A survey of over 1,000 theatre graduates asked respondents 19 questions about their theatre education and their current employment. Questions ranged from simple demographics to detailed specifics regarding where they were working and how happy they were with their current employment.

The cost of a theatre degree and the number and types of jobs in the theatre industry have changed significantly over the past few decades. The point in time when a participant graduated and began their career journey informed the questions in the study. The majority of participants (75%) were in the early years of their careers. Mid-career participants comprised 22% of the population, while 3% of participants could be identified as late career (Figure 1.1).

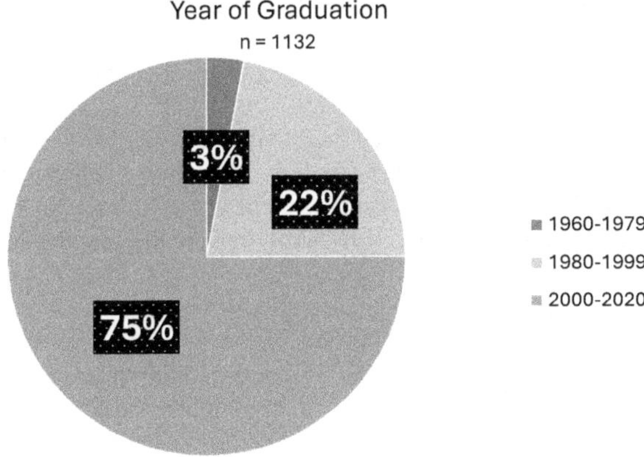

Figure 1.1 Participants by year of graduation.

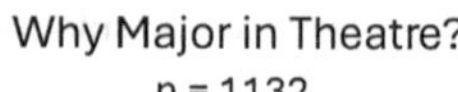

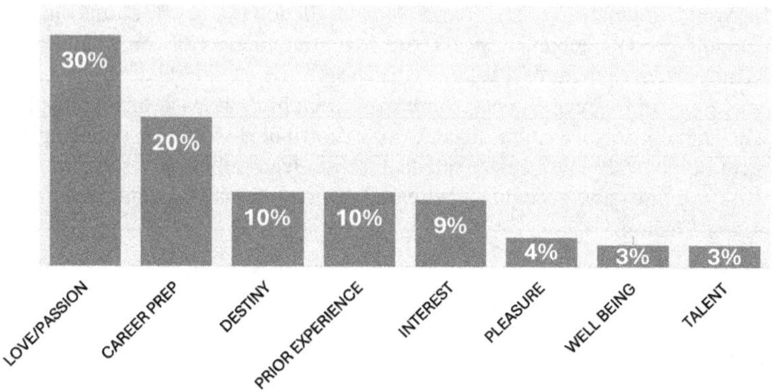

Figure 1.2 Why participants majored in theatre.

Understanding why participants chose to major in theatre offered context for later questions regarding employment satisfaction. The reasons for choosing to major in theatre were varied and sometimes surprising ranging from emotionally driven motivations like love and passion to the practical perspective that this degree (often combined with another) would help equip them to enter the job market. Choosing a major is often one of the earliest and most important decisions for a college student as it maps a curricular path and provides or denies permissions for some courses. This was an open-ended qualitative question allowing participants to describe the reasons in their own words. Coding their answers yielded the following results (Figure 1.2).

Participants provided a range of answers but passion for the field was the top choice at 31%. Those whose answers fell into this category expressed a degree of emotional intensity in their decision. "I truly loved theatre and it was the only place I felt like I belonged." For these participants, there was no other choice – this was the course of study that would bring them the most joy. Some parents recognized their child's passion for theatre and supported the wish to study theatre in college, "My parents encouraged me to pursue Drama." Others saw that standing in the way of this dream might result in resentment and unhappiness, "My family realized I wouldn't be happy if I didn't pursue it."

The second category that dominated survey answers was career preparation at 20%. For those planning to work in the field, this makes sense. It is not necessary in the United States to have a degree in theatre to work in the entertainment industry, but it can help. They recognized that by studying theatre in college, they could learn more about skills like acting, directing, voice, movement, stage management, design, playwrighting, and play analysis – all important for a theatre career. These graduates made a determined decision for a considered future, "in order to have a career in theatre arts." Some participants felt their degree was unnecessary for career preparation, "I learned almost half of what I use today from student productions, internships, apprenticeships, etc. rather than in a classroom," while others who chose a theatre major were not necessarily seeking a career in the theatre. They were most interested in the multidisciplinary nature of theatre study, "Theatre continues to broaden my worldview and teaches me valuable skills like entrepreneurship, the importance of collaboration, and understanding divergent thinking." These comments indicated that these graduates understood how the skills acquired with a theatre degree did not limit one to a career in the theatre but provided abilities applicable to several disciplines.

Some participants chose to major in theatre because they saw this as their destiny, as though the decision had been made early in life, "Don't remember ever making a decision…it just always was…." Prior experience with theatre played a large role for many participants, whether on the stage or in the audience. "I grew up seeing theatre and did lots of theatre in high school." Some who participated in theatre activities in high school found an important place of belonging when they needed it the most. "Theatre gave me a community when I had none and a purpose." Others saw theatre as an opportunity to reach out and help others, "Art can be used as a medium of social change and justice." A recurring theme from several participants was the importance of their double major, "I graduated as a double major in Theatre and Marketing."

The survey asked participants if they had chosen the degree intending to work professionally in the theatre. Most of the theatre graduates in the study (79%) chose the degree with this intent. A small number of survey participants (4%) majored with no intention of a theatre career, while 17% were not certain that a professional theatre career was their destination (Figure 1.3).

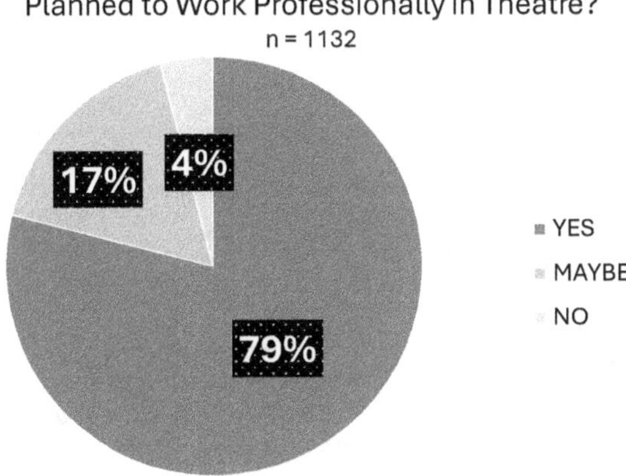

Figure 1.3 Whether participants planned to work professionally in the theatre.

To better understand this data, I examined answers from the final question of the survey. Some participants from each of the three categories (*Yes, No, Maybe*) wished that educators had provided more road maps for possible employment, including classes on budget management and the basics of the job application process, "I do wish my degree had better prepared me for the business side of things in theatre/film etc." [*Maybe*]. Recognizing that some students choose to major in theatre intending to work professionally in the industry is important for educators as most graduates will end up working in other fields at some point in their career. Educators can help prepare graduates to embrace the possibility of other career paths and to see a career shift as an opportunity rather than a failure.

In summary

Theatre graduates begin their academic journey with hopes and dreams and may choose this degree because they love the practice of theatre. They may have determined that a theatre degree is the next best step toward a theatre career and hope this course of study will replicate the emotional or social value of the degree in their future employment experiences. A few may have no expectations of a future in theatre at all. With rising tuition costs and current inflation rates, a college degree is most often viewed as an investment in future employment. The theatre market is oversaturated with far more applicants than there are openings, and it may be difficult for graduates to find an opportunity to work professionally in the theatre. Career satisfaction can be complicated for arts graduates who sometimes choose passion for the field over monetary gain. A career in the arts will come with trade-offs, but despite the challenges and the expense, some students will choose to major in theatre, and a theatre degree will help them find a job, or several jobs over the course of their careers.

Notes

1 Carnevale, A. P., Rose, S. J., & Cheah, B. (2011). *The college payoff: Education, occupations, lifetime earnings.* Center on Education and the Workforce, Georgetown University.
2 Abel, J. R. & Deitz, R. (2019, June 3). *The cost of college continues to climb.* Liberty Street Economics. https://libertystreeteconomics.newyorkfed.org/2019/06/the-cost-of-college-continues-to-climb.html
3 Carnevale, A. P. (2016). *Credentials and competencies: Demonstrating the economic value of postsecondary education.* Center on Education and the Workforce, Georgetown University.
4 Rossi, A. (Director). (June 13, 2014). *Ivory Tower* [Film]. Samuel Goldwyn Films, 55:05.
5 Bridgstock, R., & Cunningham, S. (2016). Creative labour and graduate outcomes: Implications for higher education and cultural policy. *International Journal of Cultural Policy, 22*(1), 10–26.

6 Freeman, J. (2012). Drama at a time of crisis: Actor training, performance study and the creative workplace. *International Journal of Education & the Arts, 13*(4), 1–22.
7 Yao, Y. (2022, March 3). *Humanities and the battle of the university*. The Harvard Crimson, Harvard University.
8 SNAAP. (n.d.). 2015, 2016, & 2017 Aggregate frequency report. *Strategic National Arts Alumni Project (SNAAP)*. https://snaaparts.org/uploads/downloads/Reports/SNAAP-151617-Aggregate-Report.pdf
9 Leach, J. (2014). Cultural power and the role of the humanities. *The Journal of Arts Management, Law, and Society, 44*(1), 47–56.
10 National Endowment for the Arts. (2018, March 6). *The arts contribute more than $760 billion to the U.S. economy new findings released on economic impact of arts*. https://www.arts.gov/news/press-releases/2018/arts-contribute-more-760-billion-us-economy
11 US Bureau of Labor Statistics. (n.d.). https://www.bls.gov/ooh/entertainment-and-sports/actors.htm#tab-6 (accessed April 4, 2024).
12 US Bureau of Labor Statistics. (n.d.). https://www.bls.gov/ooh/entertainment-and-sports/producers-and-directors.htm (accessed April 4, 2024).
13 Pink, D. H. (2005). *A whole new mind: Moving from the informational age to the conceptual age*. Riverhead Books.
14 Pink, D. H. (2004). The MFA is the new MBA. *Harvard Business Review, 82*(2), 21–22.
15 Selingo, J. J. (2013). *College (un) bound: The future of higher education and what it means for students*. Houghton Mifflin Harcourt.
16 National Leadership Council for Liberal Education and America's Promise. (2007). *College learning for the new global century*. https://nsee.memberclicks.net/assets/docs/KnowledgeCenter/IntegratingExpEduc/BooksReports/82.2.%20college%20learning%20for%20the%20new%20global%20century.pdf
17 Selingo, J. J. (2013). *College (un) bound: The future of higher education and what it means for students*. Houghton Mifflin Harcourt.
18 Anderson, M., & Dunn, J. (Eds.). (2013). *How drama activates learning: Contemporary research and practice*. A&C Black.
19 Robinson, K. (2011). *Out of our minds: Learning to be creative*. John Wiley & Sons.
20 Clifton, D. O., Anderson, E., & Schreiner, L. A. (2006). *StrengthsQuest: Discover and develop your strengths in academics, career, and beyond* (2nd ed.). Gallup Press.
21 Lipka, S. (2019). Preparing students for 21st-century careers (Roundtable Report). *The Chronicle of Higher Education*.
22 Throsby, D., & Zednik, A. (2011). Multiple job-holding and artistic careers: Some empirical evidence. *Cultural Trends, 20*(1), 9–24.
23 Comunian, R., Faggian, A., & Li, Q. C. (2010). Unrewarded careers in the creative class: The strange case of bohemian graduates. *Papers in Regional Science, 89*(2), 389–410.
24 Caves, R. E. (2000). *Creative industries: Contracts between art and commerce (No. 20)*. Harvard University Press.
25 Ball, L., Pollard, E., & Stanley, N. (2010). *Creative graduates creative futures*. Institute for Employment Studies.
26 Lindemann, D. J., & Tepper, S. J. (2012). Painting with broader strokes: Reassessing the value of an arts degree--based on the results of the 2010 Strategic National Arts Alumni Project. Special Report 1. *Strategic National Arts Alumni Project*.
27 Bridgstock, R., & Cunningham, S. (2016). Creative labour and graduate outcomes: Implications for higher education and cultural policy. *International Journal of Cultural Policy, 22*(1), 10–26.
28 Pink, D. (2005). *A whole new mind: Moving from the informational age to the conceptual age*. Riverhead Books.

29 Spencer, A. C. (2019). *Forging pathways to purposeful work: The role of higher education*. Gallup.
30 Adamuti-Trache, M., Hawkey, C., Schuetze, H. G., & Glickman, V. (2006). The labour market value of liberal arts and applied education programs: Evidence from British Columbia. *Canadian Journal of Higher Education, 36*(2), 49–74.
31 Praskova, A., Creed, P. A., & Hood, M. (2015). Career identity and the complex mediating relationships between career preparatory actions and career progress markers. *Journal of Vocational Behavior, 87*, 145–153. https://doi.org/10.1016/j.jvb.2015.01.001
32 Hagmaier, T., Abele, A. E., & Goebel, K. (2018). How do career satisfaction and life satisfaction associate? *Journal of Managerial Psychology, 33*(2), 142–160.
33 Gopalan, N., & Pattusamy, M. (2020). Role of work and family factors in predicting career satisfaction and life success. *International Journal of Environmental Research and Public Health, 17*(14), 5096.

2 Patterns of employment

The career path for a theatre graduate is complex and variable. Multiple factors can guide where and how an aspiring theatre artist finds work. To help us better understand this complexity, let us examine the career trajectories of four fictional but representative theatre graduates. These abbreviated scenarios offer a glimpse into a few of the possible employment pathways for contemporary theatre graduates.

Four employment scenarios

We will begin with Pat. Pat knew from an early age that she wanted to be an actor. Following graduation, Pat moved to Chicago to begin establishing her career. The first few years trying to break into the business were challenging. She cobbled together a collection of jobs: barista at the local coffee shop, running food for a delivery company, and serving as a simulated patient at one of the big hospitals in the city. All of these jobs were chosen for their adaptability. When Pat had a big audition or a short-term performance opportunity, she could drop her temporary work, focus full time on theatre activities, and return to her temporary work when her theatre employment ended. By her seventh year in the Windy City, Pat had a breakthrough, landing a lead role in a national tour of a Broadway musical. This breakthrough gave her the exposure she needed to attract the interest of a theatrical agent who agreed to help her book future performance contracts. When the 12-month national tour ended, Pat qualified to become a member of Actor's Equity Association, the professional union for actors and stage managers, and an important benchmark in a performance career. Rather than slinging coffee or delivering food between performance contracts, Pat now engaged in periodic film and television work. After several years of struggle, Pat was now a full-time working artist. Although she still had to hustle to find theatre employment, her membership in professional unions provided enough health insurance coverage for her to get by.

Greg went to college to become a set designer. He had always been a talented visual artist, and a high school mentor encouraged him to continue his

DOI: 10.4324/9781003520023-3

art studies in college. When Greg graduated, he moved to New York City, recognizing that this geographic location was the epicenter of the work he hoped to do on Broadway. He began his career assisting other set designers, first at smaller theatres, and then Off-Broadway. During the early years of his career, Greg painted houses to make ends meet. Eventually, he began to land design contracts and found himself flying across the country regularly to design productions. A few years into his career, Greg married and decided to have children. With this important shift in life circumstances, he knew something had to change. The itinerant life of a freelance designer would not be good for his family. He went back to school and got an MFA in design from New York University. With his graduate degree in hand, he applied for and landed an Assistant Professorship at Rutgers University. Greg now teaches during the day, mentors students in the evening, and periodically designs shows for theatres across the river in New York City. The stable salary afforded by a university position allowed Greg to feel comfortable starting a family, and he continues to stay engaged with the theatre industry through his teaching and professional work. This blended career was the right fit for Greg's new life circumstances.

Dallas never had an interest in performance or design. Highly organized and socially shy, Dallas found stage management in high school. They excelled in organization and time management and were a natural leader and a gifted problem solver. While studying theatre in college, Dallas managed 15 productions, a record for their particular theatre department. Following graduation, Dallas decided to remain in their hometown of Seattle, Washington. Seattle had a thriving theatre scene, and Dallas found employment in the field almost immediately. Their talent earned them a reputation for excellence, and Dallas found that within two years, they could pick and choose stage management contracts. Dallas had more work than they could handle, and although they had initially enjoyed the job, they were now experiencing burnout. Dallas decided they didn't want to stage manage anymore. They didn't want to work in the theatre at all. They applied for and won a position as a project manager at a tech company. Initially, the shift required a lot of adjustment, but within a few short months, Dallas was applying their exceptional time management, organization, and team leadership skills and advancing through the company ranks. Although no longer a stage manager, Dallas continues to use the creative skills they acquired with their theatre degree in their current position.

Jordan wanted to be a director. In college, she took advantage of every opportunity to assist other directors or to direct a production herself. When she graduated, she moved to New York City and began the process of trying to find a job in theatre. She visited numerous theatre companies in New York, offering to assist for free, but she was among many recent graduates who had made the same pitch. After three years of trying to find a foothold in the industry, Jordan quit. She was tired of the grind of a theatre career. She went back to school and got a law degree. She now works as a defense attorney for a moderately sized law firm in New York. Although not the path she had hoped to take with her career, she admits that she often engages some of the skills she used in college as she researches and strategizes to prepare and present a defense for her clients. She no longer practices theatre, nor does she attend theatre. Although she chose to leave the field for another form of employment, she has no regrets about getting a theatre degree.

The trajectory of a career in the arts

As the examples above demonstrate, an arts career takes time to establish. Patterns of employment and the needs of the artist can shift over time and may change how they choose to support themselves. Early in their career, many artists engage in temporary work to pay the bills. As we saw with Pat, this may involve waiting tables, working as an office temp, or driving for Uber. Designers, directors, actors, playwrights, and other aspiring theatre professionals begin a journey in which they attempt to sell their skills to prospective employers via a relentless audition/submission process or serving as an artistic assistant for little to no pay. These engagements are important as they have the potential to lead to more remunerative opportunities, but they do not pay the rent. Therefore, young artists must supplement their income with another job or jobs. This second job, often called a "day job" in the theatre (even though some of these activities may occur at night), needs to provide some flexibility so that an aspiring artist may take advantage of arts work when the occasion arises.

Opportunities early in the career may be rare and are often poorly paid. Underemployment is recognized by many artists as part of the contract for those endeavoring to establish an artistic career. Those struggling through these early years believe that their monetary, social, and professional sacrifice will eventually lead to more stable and prosperous employment as they build their artistic reputation and become more networked within the industry. Despite the challenges presented by overwork and underemployment, some artists believe that their work at Starbucks or Denny's, although temporary, has value and that these efforts are contributing to their careers.[1] Other artists find work outside of the arts industry demeaning and confusing. They did not attend university for the opportunity to wait tables or drive for a ride-share company and having to engage in these non-artistic endeavors interferes with their professional identity. The transition time following graduation can be difficult for some, eroding self-confidence and pushing them to question their decision to major in an arts subject in the first place.

The situation and concerns for a mid-career artist are different from those just beginning their professional journey. If we identify early career as roughly the first ten years following graduation, then mid-career could be recognized as 10–20 years post-graduation. At mid-career, the arts graduate has had ample time to engage in the hard work of establishing themselves in the field, building a reputation, and creating a professional network. This may be the most common time in an arts career when graduates decide to shift fields or remap their employment. Professional identities for artists shift and evolve in response to life's circumstances.[2] As we saw with Greg, starting a family may change priorities. An aspiring artist may find themselves caring for an elderly parent or struggling to negotiate a new disability. In some cases, they may become tired of the struggle to make ends meet and choose an employment path that offers more money and stability.[3] According to a recent SNAAP Special Report investigating which arts graduates remain in an arts career, artists who trained in more than one arts discipline tended to stay in the business longer than those who specialized in only one area of their field.[4] Expanding the knowledge base to include more than one area of specialization could provide graduates with more flexibility and adaptability, allowing them to shift their employment according to the work currently available. Because the arts job market is always oversaturated with prospective employees, this flexibility may offer a logistical advantage. According to the SNAAP report, as of 2020, 78% of arts graduates expected to freelance at some point in their career, and 84% expected to work outside of the arts.[5]

Those artists who stay in the field into their late careers have managed to establish themselves professionally or to create a hybrid career that combines their artistic practice with other arts adjacent work that can fill in the gaps when times are lean. Actors who work in the profession their entire career are usually located in a large city like New York, Los Angeles, or Chicago. They may supplement their artistic work in a variety of ways including using unemployment benefits between engagements or choosing to live in subsidized housing. Designers who have spent a career freelancing in the theatre may supplement their work with occasional industrial designs, or periodic work in the film industry. Playwrights and dramaturgs may find themselves relying on part-time work in film and television. Late-career artists have either found consistent success in gaining arts employment or have made peace with the precarity of the profession by supplementing their artistic endeavors in other ways. Some, like Dallas and Jordan, may have chosen to leave the field for another employment sector. Those who have stayed in the theatre for their entire careers are exceptional and certainly to be admired for their resourcefulness and tenacity.

Seeking employment in a shifting job market

An examination of the trajectory of an arts career reveals some hard truths: a life-long career in the arts requires compromises, and many arts graduates who begin a career as an artist will choose to shift to another field or will create a hybrid career that includes at least some work outside of the arts. This situation is not exclusive to the arts. A paper published by Humphreys and Kelly in 2014 identified that 40% of all college graduates end up working in a field different from their course of study.[6] Creative thinking and creative problem-solving are currently in high demand throughout the employment sector. These skills are embedded in the learning outcomes for arts graduates but are not always included in the curriculum for other disciplines on campus.[7] This is unfortunate as many organizations are seeking creative people to hire but are struggling to find them.[8] The recent interest in add-on certification in various subjects has helped graduates in some fields broaden their knowledge base, but employers emphasize that specialization and pedigree are less useful than demonstrated ability.[9]

Burning Glass Technologies, a leading research institute focused on gathering data on contemporary work patterns, recently identified a trend toward hybrid work that requires a multidisciplinary knowledge base. These jobs have been labeled "very high" or "high" in complexity and currently represent 12% of the workforce. They also pay 20% to 40% more than their traditional counterparts. As artificial intelligence continues to advance and influence the job market, those who specialize in tasks that can only be done by people become ever more valuable.[10] According to Burning Glass, these hybrid jobs are hard to fill, as they require four primary skills to qualify for employment: (1) work with digital technology, (2) the ability to engage in data analysis, (3) business management, and (4) thinking like a creative. Should an arts graduate wish to qualify for one of these elite positions, additional education in business, technology, and data analysis would make them an attractive candidate while a computer science major would need to supplement their training with study in fields like music, dance, or theatre.

An undergraduate education in theatre that includes rudimentary business skills and proficiency in digital technology opens many doors for future employment. According to Michelle Weise, author of *Long life learning: Preparing for jobs that don't even exist yet*, the combination of digital and soft skills is important for the employment market of the future.[11] The interpersonal, communication, creative problem-solving, and adaptability skills provided by a theatre degree are currently in high demand. Because arts graduates often gravitate toward less traditional forms of employment, they are well-positioned to step into jobs that are only just emerging in response to new market needs. Several of these jobs require some proficiency in both art and science, further reinforcing the call for multidisciplinary education. In 2017, Michael Litt explained that the tech industry liked to hire humanities majors because they were better at providing the context behind innovation and discovery. According to Litt, a science or engineering graduate can tell you what it is, but one needs an arts or humanities graduate to identify what it means.[12]

One example of a new job responding to the current employment needs is the localization engineer. Localization engineers assist companies who are moving digital technologies to a new cultural environment. If a film company wants to release an American movie in Japan, for example, they need more skills than just translation. Someone must monitor cultural sensitivities in subtitling, dubbing, merchandising, and distribution. Providing an understanding of cultural context and sensitivity to the needs of the local population is the job of the localization engineer. Amazon and Nintendo are but two of the many companies involved in international business that have begun to hire people in these positions.[13] Recently, companies have begun hiring AI prompt engineers. Having an artificial intelligence tool can be helpful when conducting research, writing standard documents, or brainstorming ideas. These tools, which require humans to activate the massive information they contain, can only be helpful if the user constructs the question in a useful way. Properly constructed questions can help train AI tools to better serve the needs of a business saving time and money and maximizing the opportunities AI software can provide. To serve as a prompt engineer one must possess a combination of linguistic, interpersonal, creative thinking, and digital technology skills.[14]

Where are arts grads working?

The current systems for measuring employment amplify the complexity of tracking the employment patterns of theatre graduates. These graduates may be working several jobs at once making their primary source of income challenging to identify, or they may choose to shift to another field entirely making them hard to find. Part of the problem is how economists sort and categorize employment data. Those who study employment patterns often rely on census data or labor statistics for their research. These tools capture big-picture information like who works where, how much they earn, and an industry's relative contribution to the economy and the job market. In the United States, these data are tracked and gathered by the Bureau of Labor Statistics (BLS), a government organization that uses broad categories to measure employment. The BLS tracks arts employment using the category "27-0000 Arts, Design, Entertainment, Sports, and Media Occupations (Major Group)."[15] This designation includes actors, directors, designers, and producers, all theatre and film related categories, but it also includes court reporters, umpires, and window trimmers. If one looks more carefully at a specific job category like "Actors," one finds only semi-helpful information about real employment numbers. Here, we are informed that among the top-paying jobs for an actor (just below those in film and television) are Accounting, Bookkeeping, and Payroll, a possible but unlikely match for a new theatre graduate. More helpful than the BLS is the O*NET database, a detailed and comprehensive collection of employment information in the United States.[16] The O*NET website provides an array of job categories that fall more logically together under the umbrella of Arts and Entertainment. Although court reporters have disappeared in the O*NET arts category, umpires and other odd matches remain, including an array of jobs in the gambling industry. What O*NET does provide that the BLS website does not is an interactive relationship with the user, allowing one to explore the financial implications of certain career decisions, given the current marketplace. The BLS and the O*NET database are doing their best to track arts employment, but they do not accurately capture the employment patterns of many arts graduates. It is common for artists to work more than one job at a time, particularly at the beginning of a career, and because these data sets only identify one source of income, arts labor may be misrepresented or undercounted.

In the late 1980s and early 1990s, scholars began to develop a strong interest in the economics of the arts labor market.[17] The contributions of the arts to local and national economies were becoming an important consideration for policymakers. Creative types appeared to be the key to innovation and global competition, and researchers wanted to find a way to accurately measure their employment and its economic impact.[18] From these efforts emerged the concept of the Creative Industries (CI).[19] Researchers were keen to better understand the CI and to learn the nature of these creative jobs. Although the concept of CI may vary slightly from region to region,[20] early research designated 15 industries as belonging to the creative sector: (1) Advertising, (2) Architecture, (3) Art, (4) Crafts, (5) Design, (6) Fashion, (7) Film, (8) Music, (9) Performing Arts (Theatre/Opera/Dance/Ballet), (10) Publishing, (11) Research and Development, (12) Software, (13) Toys and Games (excluding video games), (14) TV and Radio, and (15) Video Games.[21] These categories covered a wide range of creative activities and represented one of the first attempts to identify creative labor. This was an important first step, as these arts-specific categories could now be included in census and labor surveys. But this did not solve the primary problem for tracking arts labor – that many of those working in the CI were engaged in a variety of jobs with differing sources of income, and that the census and labor surveys they were using to gather data could only track one income source.[22]

The first attempt to solve this tracking problem was the Department of Culture, Media, and Sport's (DCMS) *Creative Industries Mapping Study* released in 1998.[23] In this study, the U.K. government used census data to recategorize certain types of employment as "creative" allowing researchers to capture arts employment that aligned with standard industry codes. Over the next three years, the DCMS continued to refine these categories, working hard to properly identify creative work and capture it in a format that was useful for all. Unfortunately, the ongoing improvements in category designation made it impossible to track the data over time as the categories continued to shift and evolve so that the definitions in one data set failed to match those for the following year.[24]

In 2003, the DCMS reframed their employment categories, shifting their emphasis from standard government industry codes to occupational designations, following the lead of researchers in Hong Kong and Ontario. This allowed them to capture employment data from identifiable CIs but also included creative activity that was happening in non-CIs. This form of

		Creative and Cultural Sector	
		Yes	No
Cultural and Creative Occupations	Yes	**Specialist Creative Workers** *(creative occupations in creative sectors)*	**Embedded Creative Workers** *(creative occupations in non-creative sectors)*
	No	**Support Workers** *(non-creative occupations in creative sectors)*	**(un-named in the Creative Trident)** *(non-creative occupations in non-creative sectors)*

Figure 2.1 The Creative Trident

employment, a graphic designer working at a law firm, for example, was labeled "embedded creative employment." By broadening these classifications, the DCMS identified 75% more creative employment than with their initial mapping studies, employment that had not previously been counted as belonging to the creative sector.[25] This improved approach to mapping creative workers was a significant step forward, but economists discovered that one segment of the creative workforce was missing. They had found a way to capture creative workers employed in creative sectors and creative workers employed in non-creative sectors, but what about non-creative workers employed in the creative sector? These important jobs (the executive director of the museum, the bookkeeper for the art gallery, the camera repairman for the film studio, as examples) were not included as belonging to the creative sector because of their occupational classifications, even though they were unquestionably working in a CI. To solve this problem and capture this additional employment population, Higgs and his colleagues developed a new measurement tool called the Creative Trident (Figure 2.1).[26]

A trident is a three-pronged spear. In the figure above, the three prongs of the trident are represented by the three sectors of creative employment. When cross-comparing possible creative occupations against the types of work in the creative sector, we see three primary categories: (1) Specialist Creative Workers (artists, singers, filmmakers, etc.), (2) Embedded Creative Workers (graphic designers, social media specialists, public speaking coaches, etc.) and (3) Support Workers (administrators, cleaning staff, accountants, etc.) By "de-coupling" creative work from CIs, we broaden the net that allows us to track and capture all creative employees working in all employment sectors.[27] If we return to one of the employment examples of our fictional theatre graduates at the beginning of this chapter, we begin to recognize the complexity of tracking arts employment. Pat's early work as a barista and a food delivery driver would be considered outside of the creative sector. Her national tour with acting engagements all year long would place her in the Specialist Creative Worker category. Without the Creative Trident, Pat's work as a simulated patient would have been considered outside of the creative sector even though the job required special creative skills (acting ability). When applying the Creative Trident to Pat's employment activities, her work as a simulated patient is categorized as embedded creative labor and counted as employment in the creative sector. The ability to identify Embedded Creative Workers and Support Workers as part of the employment pool in the creative sector allowed economists, policymakers, and other research specialists to more accurately understand where arts graduates and creative artists were working. This was a big step in the right direction, but it did not go far enough in tracking the nuance of employment patterns for many creative workers.

The Creative Trident redefined

The Creative Trident was developed to help economists and policymakers better understand employment patterns for the CI. By definition, many sectors of the CI include fields that function differently from the field of theatre (architecture and publishing, for example). Additionally, the British and Australian economies, which have done the most research in this area, engage with artists, arts policy, and arts funding differently from those practices in the United States. The goal of this study was to better understand the employment patterns for theatre graduates in the United States, and therefore it is helpful to adjust the Creative Trident categories to capture those work patterns more accurately. Some scholars who laud the advancement created by the Creative Trident have recognized the limitations this model presents, particularly when trying to identify and measure the complexity of the work patterns for Embedded Creative Workers.[28] Goldsmith and Bridgstock labeled the Creative Trident as a top-down measurement tool and called for bottom-up surveys that could more accurately identify the nuance in each sector.[29] This study was designed to capture theatre employment more accurately, by utilizing a modified version of the Creative Trident tailored to the employment patterns of theatre graduates (Figure 2.2):

		Creative and Cultural Sector	
		Yes	No
Utilization of Creative Skills for Employment	Yes	**Working Artists** *(working full time in the theatre industry)*	**Shifted Career Creative Skills** *(working outside of the theatre industry applying theatre skills)*
	No	**Blended Career** *(working inside and outside of the theatre industry)*	**Shifted Career Has Left the Field** *(working full time outside of the theatre industry)*

Figure 2.2 The Modified Creative Trident

The Modified Creative Trident (MCT) offered a framework to better understand where theatre graduates were working, what that work looked like, and how a theatre education impacted that employment. The Creative Trident cross-compared creative occupations inside and outside of the creative sector. The MCT shifted those categories and cross-compared the application of the creative skills acquired with a theatre degree to employment inside and outside of the theatre industry. In the MCT, the label "creative skills" referred to those skills acquired as core components of an undergraduate theatre curriculum. The curriculum in theatre departments may vary in specifics but most departments offer classes in acting, directing, design, stage management, technical theatre, theatre history, play analysis, playwriting, movement, and voice. Each of these classes contains an array of creative skills that could be applied to a variety of employment paradigms. Rather than the three employment categories offered in the Creative Trident (Specialist Creative Worker, Embedded Creative Worker, Support Worker), the MCT provided four: (1) Working Artist (applying creative skills to full-time work in the theatre industry). (2) Blended Career (applying creative skills to work inside and outside of the theatre industry simultaneously). (3) Shifted Career/Creative Skills (applying creative skills to work outside of the theatre industry as full-time employment). (4) Shifted Career/Has Left the Field (working full time outside of the theatre industry with no direct application of the creative skills acquired with the degree). Shifted Career/Creative Skills is the closest category to Embedded Creative Worker in the Creative Trident. In this study, the MCT framework captured the employment patterns of theatre graduates who were using their creative skills directly or indirectly in their current employment but who may or may not have been working toward a full-time career in the theatre industry. Working Artist and Shifted Career/Has Left the Field categories are self-explanatory. Blended career was the most inclusive category as it was designed to capture the widest array of non-traditional employment by theatre graduates and any possible combination of theatre and non-theatre work.

It is worth taking a moment here to address cultural context and language. Many of the scholars referenced in the research for this book come from the England and Australia and are doing important work decoding and advocating for the arts communities in those locations. The field-specific language and arts employment context in the United States are distinct from those geographies. One of the most important definitions that requires cultural reframing is the term "portfolio career," regularly used by these CI scholars. In the 1990s in Britain and Australia, researchers began to identify a segment of the workforce that was engaging in multiple jobs at once. This multi-job category was labeled "the boundaryless career."[30] Seen initially as an opportunity for autonomy and freedom for some freelance employees, this new employment paradigm was a concern for organizations accustomed to a stable, salaried workforce.[31] Over time, employers began to perceive the advantage of hiring these contract employees instead of paying the expenses attached to someone with a full-time salary.[32] The term "boundaryless career" evolved to become known as a "portfolio career," so defined as it comprised multiple work activities that function as the employee's portfolio.[33] This term was applied to any freelance worker in any field, and arts scholars in the United Kingdom and Australia soon adopted the term to refer to creative workers who were engaging in multiple forms of employment.

In the United States, we initially referred to freelance employees as gig workers. The term "gig" originated from musicians who would book multiple engagements at different establishments and referred to these bookings as gigs.[34] Describing a freelance theatre career as a portfolio career can be problematic and confusing within an American context. For a corporate or government employee, a portfolio may refer to the collection of responsibilities for a given salaried position. For an artist, a portfolio is a collection of arts-based artifacts that testify to the qualifications of the artist for the artistic job to which they are applying. For an actor, the portfolio would consist of a headshot, resume, reel, and collection of monologues. For a designer, a portfolio might include a website of photographs, a collection of renderings, and several miniature models of sets they have designed. For a stage manager, it would be their collection of prompt books demonstrating their skill and experience in running a show. What would not be considered a part of a portfolio within a theatre artist's nomenclature in the United States is working at Starbucks, temporary office work, or running food for DoorDash. Because our focus here is on the employment patterns of theatre graduates in the United States, the MCT framework used the term Blended-Career rather than portfolio career. This label implied that the artist had constructed a collection of employment opportunities that were variable and adaptable. They had "blended" their arts work with their non-arts work in a paradigm that might shift as their artistic opportunities and life choices changed over time.

What the survey told us

The importance of accurately tracking employment activities for theatre graduates cannot be understated. Government policies often rely on employment statistics to determine how and where to distribute tax dollars. Universities are held accountable for the employment rates of their graduates, often relying on field-specific data to identify which programs are delivering the most attractive employment statistics. Finding a way to demonstrate that arts graduates, and theatre graduates in particular, are not only finding employment but are applying the skills acquired with their theatre degree to that employment is critically important when defending the value of theatre programs. This study gathered an array of information on employment specifics from actual theatre

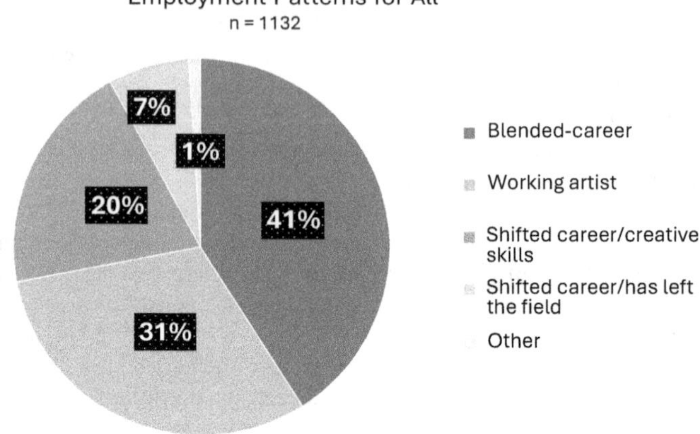

Figure 2.3 Employment patterns for all participants.

graduates, exposing the complexity and variety of employment pathways for this population.

To begin tracking the employment patterns of survey participants, I engaged the MCT, prompting participants to choose from one of four categories with a definition for each.[35] "*Working artist*=Someone whose paycheck comes entirely from work in the theatre industry." "*Blended-career*=Someone whose paychecks come from multiple sources, at least one of which is in the theatre industry." "*Shifted career/creative skills*=Someone who works outside of the theatre industry but uses creative skills as a component of job tasks." "*Shifted career/has left the field*=Someone who has left the theatre field and has shifted careers." "*Other*"=This field was included in the survey should a participant have believed their work did not fit any of these categories. The results revealed that of my population of 1,132 participants, only 31% identified as working artists. That means that 69%, more than 2/3 of all of these theatre graduates were working at least part-time outside of the field of theatre. According to the MCT, most participants (41%) engaged in a blended career, while more than ¼ of participants (27%) were working entirely outside of the field of theatre (Figure 2.3).

For some pursuing a career in the theatre, the institution of study could offer a professional advantage. Elite theatre programs like Julliard or Yale contain embedded networks that more easily open doors for a young artist. An institutional advantage did not appear to apply to our pool of participants. Most participants – almost half – attended a large public university (Figure 2.4).

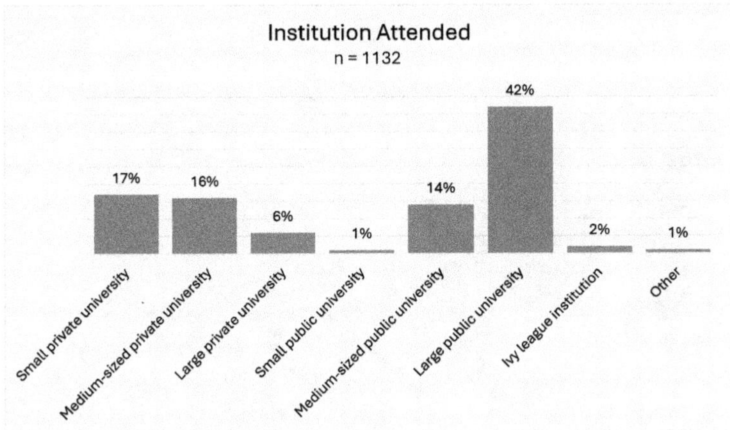

Figure 2.4 Institutions attended by participants.

Geographic location is another important influence on a theatre career. Large cities have more freelance opportunities for all disciplines in the field. The data showed the greatest concentration of participants in the *Northeast*, *Midwest*, and *West*. These areas contain the three primary cities for work in the industry in the United States: New York City, Chicago, and Los Angeles (Figure 2.5).

To determine how much graduates were earning with their employment, the survey asked them to choose one of seven income categories: \$0–\$15,000; \$15,001–\$30,000; \$30,001–\$50,000; \$50,001–\$75,000; \$75,001–\$100,000; >\$100,000; Prefer not to say. Results from this question indicated that most participants received a moderate income. A minority of participants made over \$100,000 suggesting that a robust salary is possible with a theatre degree, although unlikely for most (Figure 2.6).

Cross-comparing employment patterns and income offered some interesting insights. *Shifted/creative* showed clear growth across the salary range suggesting that those who chose to use their creative skills in another field were more likely to have a higher salary than those continuing to work in the theatre. *Shifted/left* also showed increasing representation across the income spectrum with higher numbers in the upper end of the salary range. Shifting fields was not required to earn more money but such a choice could increase earning potential (Figure 2.7).

Employment categories and income levels captured the current moment of a participant's employment pathway. Areas of interest when choosing to attend college and major in theatre identified where participants began their

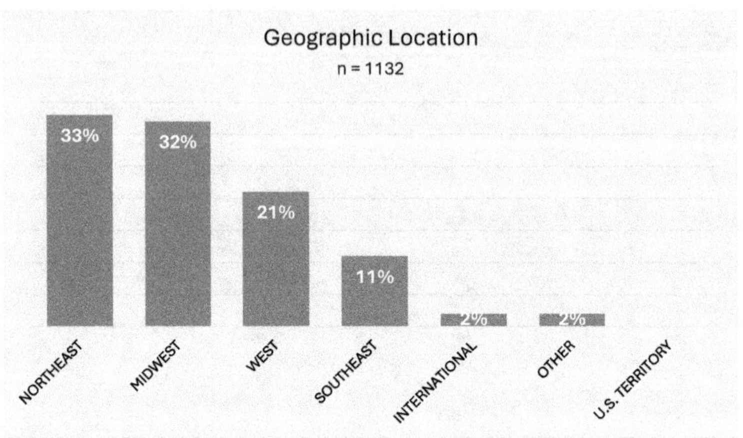

Figure 2.5 The current geographic location of participants.

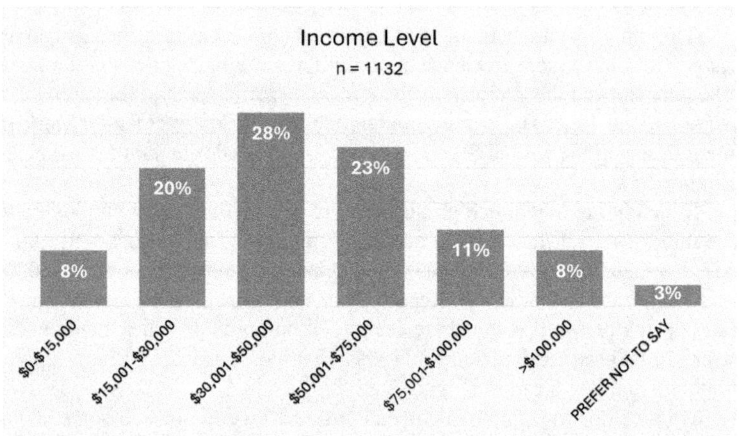

Figure 2.6 The current income level of participants.

employment journey. This information created a reference point that could be compared to their current employment reality. Becoming an actor dominated these results, an anticipated finding as performing in high school often inspires prospective students to major in theatre (Figure 2.8).

Participants began their studies with an interest in a particular career path. The survey captured where their employment journey had taken them. Each of

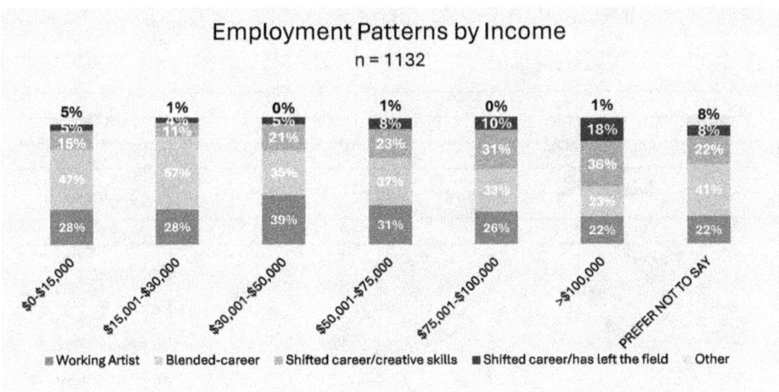

Figure 2.7 Employment patterns by income.

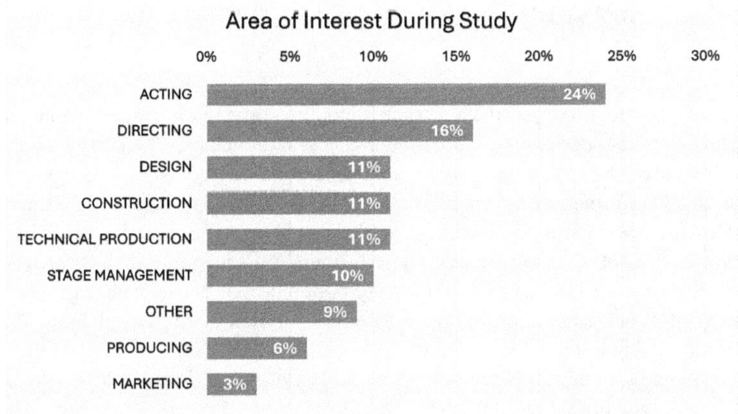

Figure 2.8 Areas of interest during theatre study.

the four pathways identified by the MCT revealed specific information regarding the complexity and variety of what participants were doing for work.

Working artists represented 31% or just under 1/3 of the participants in the study. When comparing what working artists were actually doing in the field of theatre against their initial areas of interest during their degree, we see an expected result – that the aspirations one holds as a college student will probably change post-graduation. Acting was chosen most often by participants as the initial area of interest when deciding to major in theatre. Only 11% of

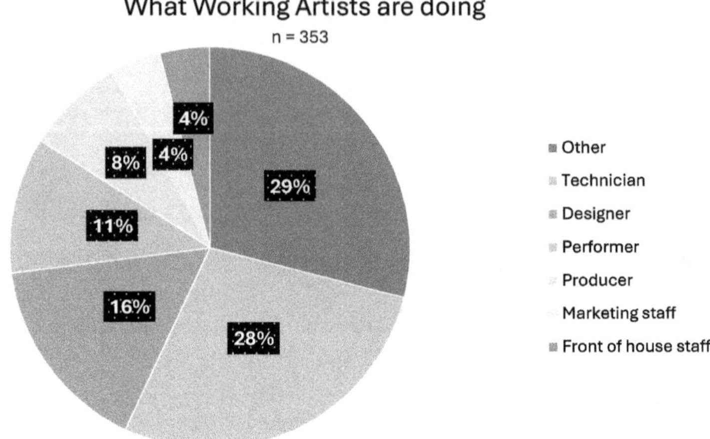

Figure 2.9 What working artists are doing.

those who identified as working artists found full-time work as actors. A larger portion of that population (28%) identified as technicians. The largest group (29%) used the *Other* category to name additional job types such as makeup artist, literary manager, or playwright. This result means that of the 353 participants who identified as working artists (out of a total population of 1,132), only 39 (11%) became professional performers. This is important information for theatre educators as 24% of the total population of participants expressed interest in becoming a professional actor during their studies, while only 3% of the total population achieved this goal (Figure 2.9).

Blended-career, Shifted/creative, and *Shifted/left* participants all engaged in non-arts work either part-time or full-time. It was revealing to examine in which industries this non-arts work was taking place. Education was the most common form of non-arts work, serving as a calling for some and a "day job" for others, a finding supported by the research.[36] Lindemann and Tepper found that more than 52% of arts graduates work as educators at some point in their careers (Figure 2.10).[37]

Other served as an opportunity for participants to provide more insight about their non-arts work. The breadth and variety of the non-arts employment indicated that theatre graduates may be found in almost any field, including engineering, medicine, and law – three fields that are considered popular with those seeking more a practical degree. The sample set below reveals only a few of the career paths chosen in each employment category (Table 2.1).

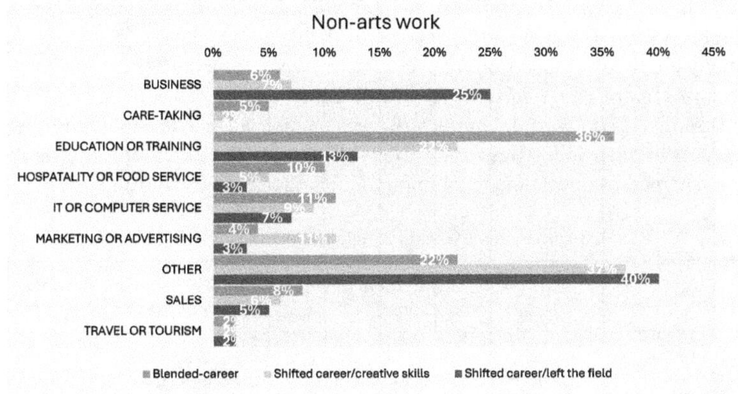

Figure 2.10 Non-arts work by employment category.

Table 2.1 Non-arts work for blended career and shifted employment participants (sample set)

	Other (please specify)
Blended career	academia broadcasting corporate education emergency medical services fundraising interior design non-profit management social work
Shifted career/creative skills	event management video editor themed entertainment corporate audio landscape architecture talk show host business affairs for television speech language pathology
Shifted career/has left the field	energy analyst finance/accounting healthcare administrator lawyer mental health/counseling public administration real estate tech entrepreneur

The employment combinations for *Blended-Career* participants were highly variable. When adding income to the data, one can see that there are many possible combinations at every income level for a theatre graduate who chooses to craft a *Blended-career* (Table 2.2).

Shifted/creative and *Shifted/left* participants had chosen to focus their careers in other industries for a variety of reasons. The need for more stability emerged as one of the most important justifications for shifting out of the

Table 2.2 Blended-career employment (sample set)

	Arts Work (employment directly related to the degree)	*Other Work (outside the field or arts-adjacent)*
\$0–\$15,000	actor choreographer/actor/director dancer director/stage manager director/dramaturg/actor musical theatre performer	Museum services fitness industry teaching artist office assistant house manager grant writing
\$15,001–\$30,000	costume designer director playwright props artisan stage manager voice over artist	banker fiction writer handyman work restaurant manager piano teacher special ed paraprofessional
\$30,001–\$50,000	artistic director choreographer comic dramaturg lighting designer stagehand	carpenter digital marketer fundraising high school theatre teacher screen printing tailor
\$50,001–\$75,000	director fight choreographer lighting designer playwright stagehand technical theatre director	business analyst nurse photographer professor social media producer software developer
\$75,000–\$100,000	actor stage manager stage director playwright singer musician	casting director government graphic designer human resources manager medicine sales manager
> \$100,000	actor/director director designer theatre professional everything backstage	arts administrator development federal government manager lighting system sales talent agent university administrator

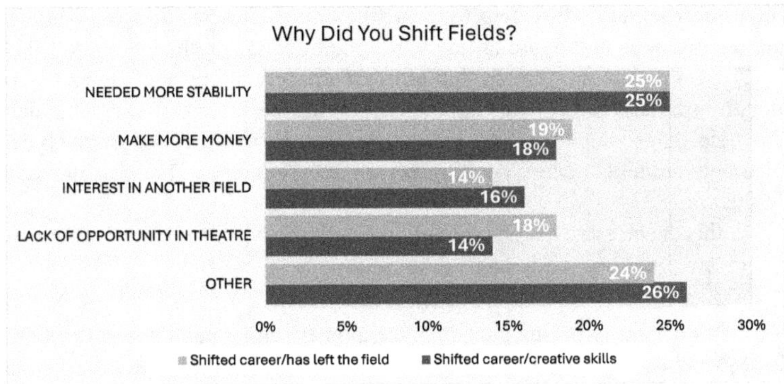

Figure 2.11 Why did participants shift out of the theatre?

theatre industry. The *Other* category revealed themes of family priorities and mental health challenges while some participants simply lost interest in the lifestyle of a theatre artist as their career progressed through time. What does not appear is a sense of regret over having studied in one field and ending up working in another (Figure 2.11).

In summary

Our four sample graduates from the beginning of this chapter offered a preview of the complexity of employment patterns for those planning to embark on a career in the theatre. For all theatre graduates, establishing a career in the industry takes time. A fractional few may break through into stardom, but these stories are exceptionally rare. More often, graduates spend years working part-time or temporary jobs in other industries to support their efforts to find theatre work. A minority of these graduates will become full-time employees in the theatre industry. The majority will either construct a blended career that includes arts and non-arts work, or they will choose to leave the field altogether.

Shifting fields has become the norm in our current dynamic job market. 40% of college graduates will end up working in a field other than their chosen major.[38] Tracking the pathways of this employment is critically important for shaping education policy and protecting vulnerable arts programs. The employment pathways of theatre graduates are complex and challenging to measure. Census databases and labor statistics fail to capture the quilted landscape of arts and non-arts work that comprises the employment patterns for a majority of theatre graduates. Those graduates who choose to leave the field and work in other industries may not be tracked at all. This underrepresentation threatens to create the impression that theatre graduates are unemployed and/or are failing to use their degrees in the job market. The MCT provided a framework that allowed me to capture and assess where theatre graduates were working and what that work looked like. This data can help shape educational policy and curriculum in theatre programs. It can also help students make a more informed decision when choosing to major in theatre.

In this chapter, we learned the following about the employment patterns of the theatre graduate participants in the study:

1 69% ended up working outside of the industry either part-time or full-time.
2 Most chose to move to geographic areas containing the three largest cities in the United States: New York, Chicago, and Los Angeles.
3 Most earned a low to moderate income with some outliers living in poverty and others earning six figures.
4 The majority hoped to become actors while only a small minority achieved this goal.
5 Of the 69% who worked outside of the industry, the most common field of employment was education, although non-arts work was found in many sectors of the economy.
6 Those who crafted a blended career were represented at all income levels in the survey.
7 Those who shifted out of the field did so for a variety of reasons but often because they were seeking more personal and financial stability.

The information provided by the survey reinforces some of what we already know: the majority of those who choose a theatre degree hoping to become working artists in the industry are unlikely to achieve their dream. It also refutes the myth that theatre graduates are destined for poverty and struggle. The majority of graduates in the study found ways to pivot their careers and gain employment either through a combination of theatre and non-theatre work or by changing fields entirely. Theatre graduates are finding work in a wide array of fields. All of this employment and how that employment relates to the theatre degree need to be counted to help protect and preserve our theatre programs.

Notes

1 Goldsmith, B., & Bridgstock, R. (2015). Embedded creative workers and creative work in education. *Journal of Education and Work, 28*(4), 369–387.
2 Ashton, D., Noonan, C., Taylor, S., & Littleton, K. (2013). Negotiating a contemporary creative identity. In D. Ashton & C. Noonan (Eds.), *Cultural Work and Higher Education*, 154–171. Palgrave.
3 Ashton, D., Noonan, C., & Ashton, D. (2013). Industry practitioners in higher education: Values, identities and cultural work. In D. Ashton & C. Noonan (Eds.), *Cultural Work and Higher Education*, 172–192. Palgrave.

4 Frenette, A., & Dowd, T. J. (2020). Careers in the arts: Who stays and who leaves? SNAAP Special Report. Spring 2020. *Strategic National Arts Alumni Project.* https://snaaparts.org/findings/reports/careers-in-the-arts-who-stays-and-who-leaves
5 Frenette, A., & Dowd, T. J. (2020). Careers in the arts: Who stays and Who leaves? SNAAP Special Report. Spring 2020. *Strategic National Arts Alumni Project.* https://snaaparts.org/findings/reports/careers-in-the-arts-who-stays-and-who-leaves
6 Humphreys, D., & Kelly, P. (2014). How liberal arts and sciences majors fare in employment: A report on earnings and long-term career paths. *Peer Review, 16*(2), 31–32.
7 Howkins, J. (2002). *The creative economy: How people make money from ideas.* Penguin UK.
8 Robinson, K. (2011). *Out of our minds: Learning to be creative*. John Wiley & Sons.
9 Gallagher, S. R. (2022). *The future of university credentials: New developments at the intersection of higher education and hiring.* Harvard Education Press.
10 Sigelman, M., Bittle, S., Markow, W., & Francis, B. (2019). *The hybrid job economy: How new skills are rewriting the DNA of the job market.* Burning Glass Technologies.
11 Weise, M. R. (2020). *Long life learning: Preparing for jobs that don't even exist yet.* John Wiley & Sons.
12 Litt, M. (2017, July 15). *Why this tech CEO keeps hiring humanities majors.* The Future of Work. https://www.fastcompany.com/40440952/why-this-tech-ceo-keeps-hiring-humanities-majors
13 Anders, G. (2017, June 25). *As movies and video games go global, new jobs open for humanities grads.* Forbes. https://www.forbes.com/sites/georgeanders/2017/06/25/as-movies-and-videogames-go-global-new-jobs-open-for-humanities-grads/#68af82911dc1
14 Craig, L. (2023, August 4). *New skills in demand as generative AI reshapes tech roles.* Tech Target. https://www.techtarget.com/searchenterpriseai/feature/New-skills-in-demand-as-generative-AI-reshapes-tech-roles?Offer=abMeterCharCount_var2
15 https://www.bls.gov/oes/current/oes270000.htm
16 https://www.onetonline.org
17 Pratt, A. C. (1997). The cultural industries production system: A case study of employment change in Britain, 1984–91. *Environment and Planning A, 29*(11), 1953–1974.
18 Throsby, D. (2008). The concentric circles model of the cultural industries. *Cultural Trends, 17*(3), 147–164.
19 Cunningham, S. (2013). *Hidden innovation: Policy, industry and the creative sector.* University of Queensland Press (Australia).
20 Hornidge, A. K. (2011). 'Creative industries': Economic programme and boundary concept. *Journal of Southeast Asian Studies, 42*(2), 253–279.
21 Howkins, J. (2002). *The creative economy: How people make money from ideas.* Penguin UK.
22 Goldsmith, B., & Bridgstock, R. (2015). Embedded creative workers and creative work in education. *Journal of Education and Work, 28*(4), 369–387.
23 Matarasso, F. (1999). *Towards a local culture index. Measuring the cultural vitality of communities.* Comedia.
24 Higgs, P., & Cunningham, S. (2008). Creative industries mapping: Where have we come from and where are we going? *Creative Industries Journal, 1*(1), 7–30.
25 Higgs, P., & Cunningham, S. (2008). Creative industries mapping: Where have we come from and where are we going? *Creative Industries Journal, 1*(1), 7–30.
26 Higgs, P., Cunningham, S., & Pagan, J. (2007). *Australia's creative economy: Definitions of the segments and sectors.* ARC Centre of Excellence for Creative Industries & Innovation (CCI).

27 Cunningham, S. (2013). *Hidden innovation: Policy, industry and the creative sector.* University of Queensland Press (Australia).
28 Cunningham, S. (2013). *Hidden innovation: Policy, industry and the creative sector.* University of Queensland Press (Australia).
29 Goldsmith, B., & Bridgstock, R. (2015). Embedded creative workers and creative work in education. *Journal of Education and Work, 28*(4), 369–387.
30 Arthur, M. B. (1994). The boundaryless career: A new perspective for organizational inquiry. *Journal of Organizational Behavior, 15*, 295–306.
31 Fenwick, T. J. (2006). Contradictions in portfolio careers: Work design and client relations. *Career Development International.*
32 Templer, A. J., & Cawsey, T. F. (1999). Rethinking career development in an era of portfolio careers. *Career Development International, 4*(2), 70–76.
33 Pollard, E. (2013). Making your way: Empirical evidence from a survey of 3,500 graduates. In D. Ashton & C. Noonan (Eds.), *Cultural Work and Higher Education*, 45–66. Palgrave.
34 Friedman, G. (2014). Workers without employers: Shadow corporations and the rise of the gig economy. *Review of Keynesian Economics, 2*(2), 171–188.
35 This language comes directly from the survey. Details about the survey and the research process may be found in the chapter on methodology at the end of the book.
36 Goldsmith, B., & Bridgstock, R. (2015). Embedded creative workers and creative work in education. *Journal of Education and Work, 28*(4), 369–387.
37 Lindemann, D. J., & Tepper, S. J. (2012). Painting with broader strokes: Reassessing the value of an arts degree--based on the results of the 2010 Strategic National Arts Alumni Project. Special Report 1. *Strategic National Arts Alumni Project.*
38 Humphreys, D., & Kelly, P. (2014). How liberal arts and sciences majors fare in employment: A report on earnings and long-term career paths. *Peer Review, 16*(2), 31–32.

3 Skills for all professions

Theatre study has the potential make a college graduate more employable. Skills that employers are currently seeking, like interpersonal communication and teamwork, are an intrinsic part of theatre pedagogy and practice. A theatre student may begin their degree intending to create a career as an actor, a designer, or a playwright only to find the reality of this career path more challenge than it is worth. Some graduates do manage to build a full-time professional career in the theatre. But many – the majority of graduates – end up blending their theatre career with another or shifting careers altogether. The skills theatre graduates learn with their degree are often applicable to other employment sectors, and some employers have begun to recruit theatre graduates knowing they bring with them a strong collection of transferable skills. Not all of the skills acquired with a theatre degree are useful in other job sectors, but many are currently actively sought by employers. The shift from a career in theatre to one in another field can transform a "failed" career as an artist into one in another field that is successful and satisfying. Here's a fictional example based on several real-life graduates I have known.

A graduate who shifted careers

Fred graduated from a mid-sized public university with a theatre major in 1993. Blessed with a strong singing voice and natural charisma, Fred dreamed of a career as a musical theatre performer. A Midwesterner who came from a family of modest means, he chose to move to Chicago rather than New York City as it was closer to home. To support himself, he registered with a temporary agency and went to work in an office using the computer skills he had taught himself at home. Within nine months, the company for whom he was doing temporary work offered him a full-time job. Auditions had proven more challenging than anticipated and the cost of living in Chicago was formidable. The full-time job included health insurance, so he said yes. The head of the professional development center at his company was impressed by Fred's friendly and ebullient personality. Soon Fred found himself in charge of all professional development classes in the corporation including but not limited

DOI: 10.4324/9781003520023-4

to computer training. Teaching was a natural for him. He loved people and found that explaining even complicated training concepts came easily. By the mid-2000s, after working for the company for just over a decade, Fred became restless. Serving as a cog in the corporate machine was beginning to wear. His aspirations for a theatre career seemed like another lifetime ago. Over drinks after work, one of his colleagues suggested that they start their own training company. Such an idea was a big step, but Fred was game to give it a try. Creating the business was a struggle at first, but within ten years the company had grown to 20 employees, Fred had married, and he and his husband were expecting their first child. Although he was not starring in a Broadway show or a major motion picture, Fred was happy with his career. Today, Fred makes enough money to pay a mortgage and take his family on nice vacations. His company now includes cultural consulting for corporations at the national and international levels. Fred's career did not follow the path he had planned in college. He began as an aspiring musical theatre performer, supported himself as a computer technician, transitioned to training director, started his own business, and is now the well-established CEO of his own company. Although a master's in business administration may have helped him on his career journey, he managed without it. He is convinced that his theatre degree provided the resilience, creativity, problem-solving, and interpersonal skills that were critically important to his success.

The predominance of shifting careers

According to the Bureau of Labor Statistics (BLS), today's average college graduate will change jobs at least 12 times over the course of their career. These changes may be driven by a waning interest in the field, shifting family requirements, or personal dissatisfaction with the workplace.[1] Employers, formerly in the power position in an application situation, are now having to find enticements to ensure that they win the hiring contest against their competition.[2] Their needs are dynamic, and many have become more interested in the adaptable skills an applicant can provide than in a college major.[3] They seek employees who are nimble and flexible and have expressed concern that graduates who present the skills required for an entry-level job in their field may lack the ability to adapt to the growing needs of the company.[4] The BLS indicates that there are currently a record number of job openings providing great opportunities for applicants. Yet, many prospective employees are struggling to find a job. A shift in employment priorities is partly to blame. Recent graduates have lost interest in beginning their careers with low-wage, hourly work. The trending use of artificial intelligence software to filter applications has also contributed to the problem. If not calibrated carefully, these algorithms can eliminate qualified candidates because their applications failed to include all of the required factors embedded in the search engine, or because the applicant used an identifier that did not match the software's data set. This leaves employers assuming there are no qualified candidates, and applicants wondering why they cannot find a job in a robust job market.[5]

Technology, in addition to complicating the application process, has accelerated the complexity of employment once an applicant has landed the job. The rise in the use of artificial intelligence promises a future we struggle to imagine. For those employees who are creative, adaptable, and innovative, the increased use of technology is an asset. Those who have failed to engage in life-long learning and to adapt to these rapid changes may soon find themselves out of a job. Michelle Weise attempted to predict future employment in her book *Long life learning: Preparing for jobs that don't even exist yet*, and recommended that applicants (and current employees) develop skills like digital literacy, creativity, resilience, and innovation.[6] The value of arts training is clear for some of our most innovative minds. According to Weise, Nobel laureates and other well-known scientists are likely to have participated in the arts or to have a craft-based hobby.[7] They recognize that engaging in activities like painting, woodworking, or playing an instrument can supplement their analytical thinking and encourage creative thought. Innovation is central to almost every field today, and arts training can provide the fundamental skills needed to think differently and see old problems in new ways. Today tech industry employees must demonstrate skills in written and oral communication, building strong professional relationships, working in a team, and listening effectively, all transferable skills that are often unavailable or underutilized in a math or science major.[8] Managers have identified the following deficits in current applicants for their positions: critical thinking/problem-solving (60% of applicants demonstrate a deficit in this skill), writing (44%), communication (46%), public speaking (39%), and interpersonal skills/teamwork (36%). They consider each of these skills, all available in an arts education, essential to good job performance.[9]

The importance of transferable skills

"Soft skills" is a term sometimes used to refer to a collection of abilities that are harder to measure than skills like programming, data analysis, and second language acquisition. Some researchers object to the term soft skills as it implies "agreeable," while "hard skills" indicates effort.[10] Other terms used in this context include life skills, behavior-based skills, human skills, survival skills, 21st-century skills, power skills, and transferable skills.[11] Any label has the potential to be illuminating or misleading, and there may be overlap from one category to another.[12] Scholars tend to agree on primary concepts and several have identified those skills they believe to be most essential to the contemporary job market.

Wagner preferred the term survival skills and identified seven important skill categories, arguing that they should be a part of every college curriculum.[13] The first is critical thinking/problem-solving which he described as the ability to analyze a situation and ask good questions. Critical thinking allows one to see the problem, while problem-solving provides possible solutions. The second is Collaboration Across Networks/Leading by Influence. This interpersonal skill defines one's ability to connect with people and persuade them to a point of view. This does not imply mere friendliness or likeability, which are also important, but the skill to read and understand others' behaviors and motivations and adapt an approach to accommodate those needs. Agility/Adaptability comprises Wagner's third survival skill. This skill allows one to quickly shift points of view in response to an emerging situation. The fourth survival skill, Initiative/Entrepreneurialism, describes the ability to take charge, self-start, and generate new ideas. The fifth skill is Oral /Written Communication. Although the ability to communicate well may seem an obvious requirement, employers complain that it appears to be missing in many college graduates. Next is Accessing/Analyzing Information. This skill is particularly important in our digital age where information is abundant, and one must work to distinguish fact from fiction and relevant data from dross. Analyzing and interpreting information is a skill artists apply in their daily work as a matter of course as factors like historical and social context, conceptual framing, and thematic analysis are core components of artistic training and practice.[14] The seventh and final survival skill is Curiosity /Imagination. This ability transforms an employee from someone passively carrying out tasks to a potential innovator and exceptional problem-solver. Wagner contended that each of these seven skills is essential for workers to thrive in our contemporary knowledge economy.

Marcel Robles preferred the term soft skills and defined them as behavioral personality-based character traits that defined one's ability as a leader.[15] Robles top soft skills were communication, courtesy, flexibility, integrity, interpersonal skills, positive attitude, professionalism, responsibility, teamwork, and work ethic.[16] Skills like courtesy, integrity, positive attitude, and work ethic make it clear why Robles saw these skills as personality-based. Paul Petrone, senior marketing manager for LinkedIn, suggested the top five skills companies need most are creativity, persuasion, collaboration, adaptability, and time management.[17] Trilling and Fadel preferred the term 21st-century skills and created a detailed and comprehensive categorization they believed to be necessary for contemporary employment success.[18] They began with three primary categories: Learning/Innovation, Digital Literacy, and Career/Life Skills. The Learning/Innovation category included critical thinking/problem-solving, communication/collaboration, and creativity/innovation. The third category, Career /Life Skills listed flexibility/adaptability, initiative/self-direction, social/cross-cultural interaction, productivity/accountability, and leadership/responsibility. In two of these categories (the first and the third) it is easy to see overlap with Wagner's survival skills and Robles and Petrone's soft skills. The second category, Digital Literacy, lived outside of the standard survival/soft skills paradigm but was endorsed as important by Michelle Weise.[19] It included information literacy, media literacy, and information/communication technologies literacy. Trilling and Fadel offered a compelling argument for digital literacy as an essential skill, an idea that several scholars have begun to champion.[20] Anthony Carnevale used O*NET's employment database[21] to ascertain which skills were trending in value in the marketplace. He found that communication and interpersonal skills were the most important for prospective employees.[22]

Although scholars do not agree on precisely which skills are most important, there are numerous commonalities, many of which are currently taught in the curriculum of an arts and humanities degree. Whether we call them soft skills or power skills, employers are united in finding them essential for their current and future employees. I will use the term transferable skills as this label indicates the ability to apply these skills within multiple employment contexts and across many job sectors.

How theatre training delivers

Although a theatre degree does not provide all of the skills an employer might be seeking, it does develop some of the highly valued transferable skills that apply to many specializations. Employers in multiple sectors have begun to recognize the value of theatre training and to incorporate the development of theatre skills into their professional development programs. Improvisation (improv), the theatrical practice of telling a story without a script, has become an important tool for learning to effectively answer questions or to speak extemporaneously. Workshops in improvisation are often a regular component of graduate training in science disciplines thanks to work by the Alan Alda Center for Communicating Science (AACS). The AACS helps scientists learn how to persuade colleagues and the public about the importance of their research.[23] Leadership training centers have begun to include improvisation as a part of their curriculum as it develops high-end listening and an openness to new ideas.[24] Medical schools are using improvisation to improve student communication and quick thinking.[25] Business schools have recently discovered the importance of improv training, recognizing that the skills this training provides are a part of almost every activity in their fast-paced, high-pressure discipline.[26]

Improvisation is but one theatre technique that may be applied to other fields. Acting classes develop high levels of interpersonal understanding and empathy. Acting training builds self-confidence, self-discipline, resilience, and adaptability – all skills that may be applied to numerous employment situations.[27] Classes in design, stage management, and text analysis, among others, embed important transferable skills like creativity, critical thinking, and professionalism that are currently sought on the job market. A 2017 Strategic National Arts Alumni Report (SNAAP) revealed that 94% of theatre majors engaged in brainstorming and the development of new ideas as a part of their degree.[28] Theatre skills are so useful that some job ads include a call for those with a theatre background. An ad in Artsearch (a commonly used digital resource for job openings in theatre) in March of 2021 read as follows:

> JERRY KELLY HEATING & AIR CONDITIONING, St Peters, MO 63304, Compensation Amount $90,000- $125,000, Open Until Filled. A challenging and rewarding opportunity for an extraordinary and ambitious individual. This rare and unique position requires the blending of two worlds. **The uncommon individual, the lone talent who is right for this, is someone who has theatrical performance acumen along with business acumen. They are equally comfortable on the theatrical stage as they are on the workforce presentation stage**. This individual must love helping people, teaching them self-confidence, working with them to be their best selves, and practicing with them to stand in front of people and successfully execute interactive presentations for audiences of one to four. As the in-house Customer Experience Trainer, this person's responsibilities include conducting skills gap analysis, preparing learning material, and evaluating results after each training session. This role requires working closely with everyone in the company who interacts with customers, identifying challenges they face on-the-job and recommending ways to increase their individual productivity.
>
> (emphasis is mine)

Although not in the theatre field, this position requires theatre skills and pays well. This is an ideal *Shifted Career/Creative Skills* opportunity. A search with the keyword "theatre" on Indeed.com for jobs in the United States earning $50,000 or more provided ads for the following possible *Blended Career* or *Shifted Career* positions: Production Coordinator, Middle School Theatre instructor, Manager of Institutional Giving, and Theatre Critic.[29] The professional theatre market may be currently oversaturated with prospective applicants, but the general employment market has ample opportunity for those who possess the transferable skills theatre training provides, and are willing to adapt that training to another field.

What theatre training looks like

Many theatre students apply the knowledge they have gained in their classroom studies via the laboratory of a live production in front of an audience. Learning how to act, design, analyze a play, create a prompt book, and other classroom skills are most useful when they are tested in a real situation. A theatre production is a highly charged, time-sensitive, complex environment that obligates students to attend to their particular job tasks while simultaneously responding and adapting to other members of the production team quickly and efficiently. Through this process, theatre students become masters at creative problem-solving, adaptability, interpersonal communication, and teamwork. Because of the complex and dynamic nature of this learning environment, it can be challenging for theatre instructors and their students to recognize and identify the specific skills students are acquiring. This is also true for the general public and the upper administration of a university. Few outside of the field of theatre understand the many hours of labor required to present a play for a live audience and how this labor contributes directly to a student's education.

Here is a list of some of the positions a theatre student might hold in a production and the tasks they would be required to perform. These job descriptions offer an overview of the complexity and interdisciplinary nature of theatre practice.

Director: The director is in charge of working with the production team to bring the show to life and present it to a live audience. The director often selects the show they wish to direct and then pitches their choice to the season selection team. If their play is chosen, they are responsible for researching every aspect of the story as well as details about previous productions of the play. The director must understand and articulate the history, the production context, the shape of the story, and the challenges the production might present to the production team. The director then works with the designers to create sets, costumes, lights, sound, and possibly projections for the production. Casting comes next as the director must choose who will play the parts. Once the casting has been determined, the director then works with the stage manager to organize rehearsals, conduct rehearsals, run technical rehearsals (where all design elements are added approximately one week prior to opening night), and check in periodically during the production run for the public to make sure all is running smoothly. If problems arise during the rehearsal process or the run of the show, the director is tasked with solving them in collaboration with members of the production team.

Actor: The actor's job is to embody the character and play the role for the public within the context outlined and rehearsed by the director. The actor must read the play, memorize the lines, intentions, and moves of the character, work with the costume designer to enable properly fitted outfits and quick changes backstage (should they be required), perform in concert and in collaboration with all other actors on stage, work with stage hands and stage managers to follow the rules and protocols required for rehearsal and performance, appear for every rehearsal and performance on time and fully prepared to work, engage and charm the audience during the performance, and improvise or fill the gap in the story should another actor forget their lines or fail to make their entrance.

Designer: The designer creates one or more components of the aesthetic world of the play. Design elements include sets, lights, sound, costumes, props, and projections. The designer reads the play and develops a point of view that will contribute to the overall conception of the production. The designer then works with the director to refine this point of view in harmony with the ideas from the entire team and begins to construct visual artifacts that help communicate these ideas. These artifacts might include hand drawings, digital sketches, objects, slide show images, or any other medium that can illustrate the ideas under discussion. Once the team determines the final design, the designer provides technical information that can be used to bring the design to life through construction. These items include drafts, renderings, elevations, computer models, miniature versions of the set, lighting or sound plots, and any other information required by carpenters, electricians, or other technicians who will be constructing the design. Designers regularly visit the shop personnel who are engaged in the construction, overseeing the process, and providing corrections when necessary. During technical rehearsals, designers work with the director to bring all elements together in preparation for opening night.

Dramaturg: The dramaturg is responsible for doing research on the play and providing historical, social, and political context for the production. The dramaturg ensures that all members of the creative team have a rich reserve of reference information as they prepare their work for the stage. The dramaturg is responsible for investigating any historical references, relationships, or artifacts described in the text and will often provide written and image-based research to answer additional questions that arise. The dramaturg is often the person who leads the post-show talkbacks with the audience or provides information to the marketing department who will sell the production to the public.

Stage Manager: The stage manager is the staff leader and communications specialist for the production. The stage manager works closely with the director to organize rehearsals and prepare the rehearsal space for the actors. The stage manager regularly engages with the designers as the designs are being constructed, flagging moments that emerge during the rehearsal process that may affect their design. The stage manager runs rehearsals according to the needs articulated by the director. The stage manager handles and is responsible for solving any problems raised by the actors. The stage manager is responsible for the safety of everyone who works on the production and must ensure that all safety protocols are in place and followed throughout the rehearsal and performance period. The stage manager provides daily reports for the entire team following each rehearsal. The stage manager runs weekly production meetings that include the designers, the director, and all technical personnel, and shares a production report that documents what was discussed with the entire team. The stage manager "calls" the show from a booth above or behind the stage. This involves using a headset to cue the sound, light, and projection board operators, any deckhands, and all other personnel involved in the performance of the production so that these elements are executed in a timely and safe fashion during the run of the show. Should an audience member experience distress, the stage manager is responsible for halting the performance, contacting emergency personnel, and determining whether the performance may continue. The stage manager is the first person in the room during rehearsals and performances and the last person to leave when the day is over.

Stagehand: The stagehand assists backstage or in the booth with sets, costumes, lights, sound, or any other production element that requires personnel for execution. A stagehand may run a light or soundboard, may move furniture between scenes, may be up on the fly rail lifting or lowering scenic elements during a transition, may run the fog machine, help an actor change costumes or put on makeup, may sweep and mop the stage before and/or after the rehearsal or performance. I use the term stagehand to cover several backstage positions that are often known by other names like board operator, dresser, and deckhand. There are usually multiple stagehands for any one production. A stagehand's job usually begins a few days before tech week and ends a few days following the close of the production. They are often responsible for taking the set apart and returning costumes and equipment to storage once the show has closed.

The details provided in all of these descriptions outline the application of a collection of transferable skills, including leadership, collaboration, teamwork, organization, creativity, problem-solving, and conflict resolution to name but a few. The interdisciplinary team-based process of learning to create a live production for the stage is rich with embodied learning. The training that supports these activities is available in most theatre programs to every student on campus.

What the survey told us

Identifying the specific learning outcomes provided by theatre training and practice is important when linking a theatre degree to employability paradigms. Each of the job tasks listed above helps a student develop an array of important transferable skills. Our challenge is to identify and measure those skills and map their value to the current job market. An evidence-based understanding of what a theatre student learns and how that knowledge may be applied to other employment sectors will encourage students in all disciplines to study theatre. To accomplish this, I selected 16 of the skills most commonly included in the standard theatre curriculum that were in alignment with the skills employers are currently seeking. These were (in alpha order): *adaptive problem-solving, collaboration, conflict management, creativity, critical thinking, cultural sensitivity, empathy, interpersonal communication, leadership, persuasion, professionalism, public speaking, self-direction, technology, time management*, and *working within a team*.

To determine a participant's perception of the relationship between theatre skills and employment, I needed them to identify which skills they had acquired through theatre study and then applied to their current employment situation. Participants were given a list of the 16 skills I had identified with a radio button next to each and asked to select which skills they had acquired with their degree by choosing all, some, or none. The results revealed *collaboration* as the top answer with a value of 90%. *Working within a team, creativity, interpersonal communication, public speaking, adaptive problem-solving, critical thinking, self-direction, time management*, and *professionalism* all showed a response of at least 70%. Some of the skills with the strongest numbers could be identified as people skills (*interpersonal communication, public speaking, working within a team*) while others might be considered creative

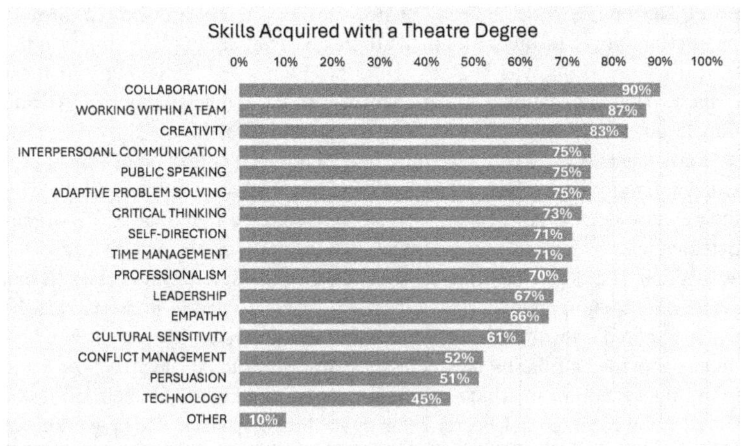

Figure 3.1 Skills acquired with a theatre degree.

(*creativity, adaptive problem-solving, critical thinking*) or appropriate for any job (*self-direction, time management, professionalism*) (Figure 3.1).

Participants also shared additional skills they had acquired with the degree that were not on the core list of 16:

- active listening
- risk-taking
- innovation
- flexibility
- confidence
- historical context
- purpose
- drive
- work ethic
- budgeting and finance
- attention to detail
- organization
- courage
- perseverance
- resourcefulness
- understanding the motivations of other people

Some of these *Other* skills – like budgeting and finance – are not present in all theatre degrees, and some participants indicated disappointment at finding the absence of at least a rudimentary finance course in their theatre curriculum. Other additional skills like confidence may emerge as a byproduct of a theatre experience and may or may not be directly transmitted through instruction. Some of the participants indicated that, although the opportunity to learn these skills was present in the program, they knew many of them already. Their educational experience was more about developing existing transferable skills rather than learning them from scratch.

Participants were able to recognize and identify the collection of skills I provided and to indicate whether they believed they had acquired these skills with their theatre degree. All of the 16 skills were selected by at least 50% of participants, except for *technology,* while 70% of participants acknowledged the acquisition of at least 10 of the 16 skills on the list. Because the list of 16 had been chosen with employer needs in mind, I next wanted to understand if the skills acquired with the degree were contributing directly to current employment. I provided a Likert scale and asked participants to consider each skill and to attribute the level to which they might be using this skill in their job tasks. Given that we learned in Chapter 2 that 69% of participants ended up working at least part-time in another field, this information was important for understanding whether their theatre skills had transferred to another employment sector. On this question, the majority of participants (65%) indicated that they used their theatre training *To a great extent* in their current employment with an additional 26% using their education *To some extent*. Not everyone in the survey believed the skills acquired with their education could be directly linked to current employment but many appeared confident about the connection (Figure 3.2).

Several participants wanted to share more detailed information about the relationship between their degree and their employment and did so in the final open-ended question in the survey.[30]

- "Most of my employers have greatly appreciated my flexibility, my improvisational skills, my public speaking, and my professionalism" [*To a great extent*]
- "One employer said that theatre professionals have good energy, charisma, and know how to talk to people" [*To a great extent*]
- "The transferable skills I learned can be implemented anywhere and I've been told several times, 'I love hiring theatre people. They don't whine about the small stuff and are so good in teams'" [*To a great extent*]
- "I have had multiple employers tell me they hired me in a non-theatre job because they know theatre majors to be especially good communicators, leaders, and critical thinkers" [*To a great extent*].
- "We found they often made the best employees. The unique blend of visualization, creative thinking, and critical thinking taught within these programs provides a valuable skill to connect the dots between what appears to be disparate concepts/ideas and figure out solutions" [*To a great extent*].

Some participants working outside of the field of theatre were compelled to identify how their degree contributed positively to their work situation.

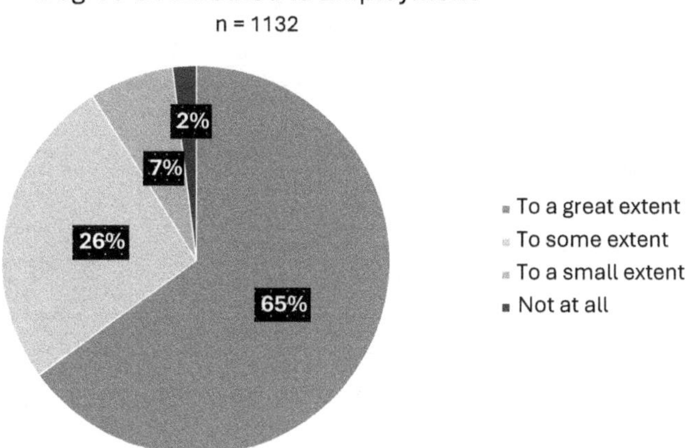

Figure 3.2 The degree's contribution to current employment.

A bank teller wrote "My theatre skills helped me just as much in that job, and I was successful because of my degree" [*To a great extent*]. Another participant shared, "Engineering finds my way of thinking (like a theatre artist) surprising and effective and it's valued and appreciated" [*To a great extent*], and another "My skills as a therapist, not to mention my interest in voice, are a direct result of my training" [*To a great extent*]. A program manager: "All my skills in that job came from my training in theatre" [*To a great extent*]. A nurse: "I know that I am a better nurse because of my theatre background, and I continue to perform in a way that is meaningful in addition to my new career" [*To some extent*]. Even entrepreneurs found the degree helpful: "My theatre degree helped me open & run my own business" [*To a great extent*]; "Putting on a production is almost exactly like starting a new company" [*To a great extent*].

Participants had identified which skills they had acquired with their degree and that their theatre training had contributed directly to their employment. Next, it was important to determine which specific skills they were using in their current employment. Participants were given a Likert scale to measure the degree to which each skill was relevant. Answers were then ranked from most to least utilized. This data revealed that most of the 16 skills were used *Almost Constantly* or *Often,* with several emerging as particularly important, including *interpersonal communication, professionalism, adaptive problem-solving, time management, collaboration, working within a team, self-direction,* and *critical thinking.* This finding was in alignment with the research on employer needs and provided strong evidence of the link between the specific skills provided by theatre training and current employment (Figure 3.3).

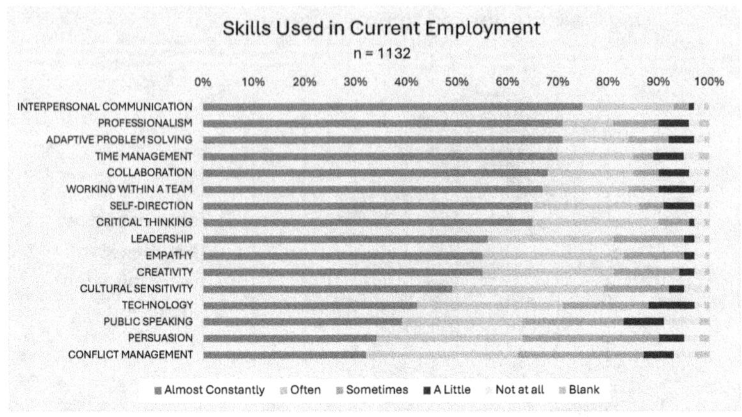

Figure 3.3 Skills used in current employment.

Other provided an opportunity for participants to share additional skills they might be using in their employment that were not on the list of 16 I provided.

- awareness of how what I am projecting into the world is being received
- organization
- engaging with others
- motivating others through creative play
- knowing how to take criticism and apply it to my work without taking it personally
- coordinating results with different stakeholders
- storytelling
- dedication
- project management
- self-marketing
- reading body language
- confidence in new situations
- risk-taking
- psychology of facial expression
- synthesizing different creative components into a coherent narrative and feel
- resourcefulness
- active listening

The data revealed that participants recognized the 16 skills on my list as belonging to their theatre education and that there was a strong link between those skills and their current employment. Because most graduates shift to another field at some point in their career, it was important to understand the relationship of skill utilization to specific employment paradigms. A life-long professional designer would have a different experience applying theatre skills to employment activities than an airline pilot or a financial planner.

Chapter 2 outlined the four primary employment patterns for graduates: *Working Artist* (working full time as a theatre professional), *Blended Career* (working part-time inside and outside of the theatre), *Shifted-Creative* (working outside of the theatre using theatre skills), and *Shifted-Left the Field* (working outside of the theatre but not consciously using theatre skills). By dividing participants into distinct employment categories and mapping their utilized skills, I identified both overlap and distinction in skills utilization between employment types. Across employment categories, the top three most utilized skills were *adaptive problem-solving, interpersonal communication,* and *professionalism.* The bottom three least utilized skills across employment categories were *conflict management, persuasion,* and *public speaking*. Working artists tended to favor *collaboration* and *working within a team* while Shifted Career/Left the Field favored *time management.* The lists for Blended Career and Shifted Career/Creative Skills were similar with small differences here and there. Although each employment category presented a distinct pattern of skill use, it was clear across categories that the majority of skills in the set of 16 were being utilized by participants *Almost Constantly* or *Often* (Figures 3.4–3.7).

In summary

College graduates who have studied within a specific field may find themselves establishing their career in another. The job market into which they will emerge upon graduation is dynamic and unpredictable. Employers need employees who are creative, innovative and committed to adapting and learning when new problems arise. A graduate's best defense is to acquire an array of adaptable skills that may be applied to a wide range of fields. Many of the critical skills that can help make them more employable are found within the curriculum of a theatre degree. Learning to act develops confidence and adaptability, design teaches creativity and context sensitivity, and stage management develops leadership, organization, and time management. Each area of specialization in theatre develops an array of transferable skills that may be applied to many fields of employment. The challenge for advocates of theatre training is to provide a clear link between a theatre education and a post-graduation career. Those who find work in the theatre and establish life-long careers as theatre professionals can easily identify the value of their theatre degree. Because most graduates will not establish full-time careers in the theatre, identifying how their theatre training may be of benefit to their employment is more challenging.

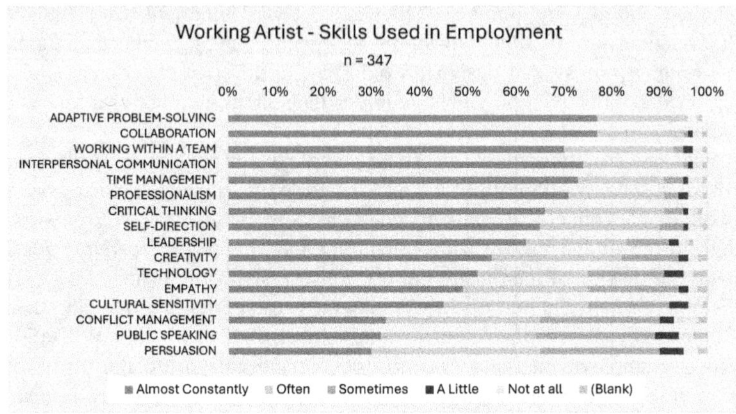

Figure 3.4 Skills used by Working Artists in current employment.

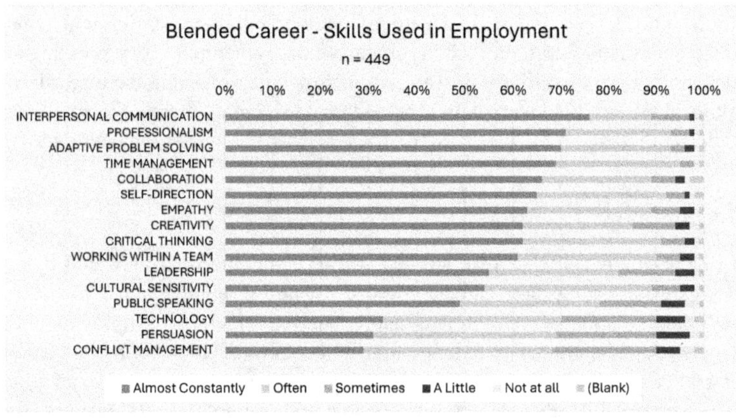

Figure 3.5 Skills used by Blended Career participants in current employment.

Participants in this study provided evidence of the link between their theatre degree and their current employment. Although not all participants agreed that the skills acquired with their theatre training were utilized in their current job tasks, the majority believed their theatre education was important to their current employment. Whether a stage director, a banker, or a nurse, many noted how studying theatre had made them better at their jobs. Skills like *interpersonal communication, working within a team*, and *adaptive problem-solving* were particularly prominent in the survey and are a strong match with those skills currently sought by employers in many fields. Participants in the survey

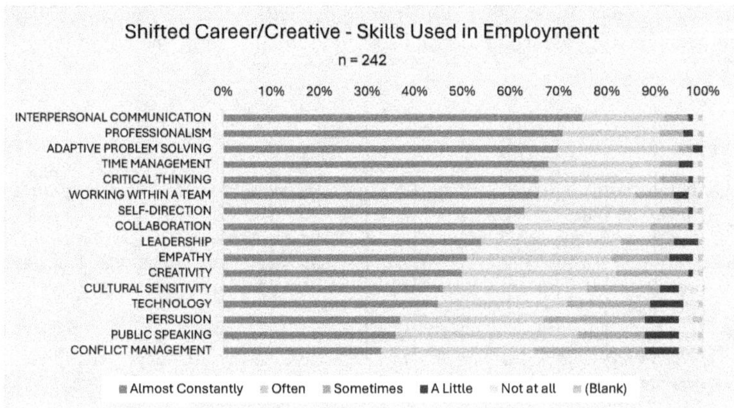

Figure 3.6 Skills used by Shifted Career/Creative Skills participants in current employment.

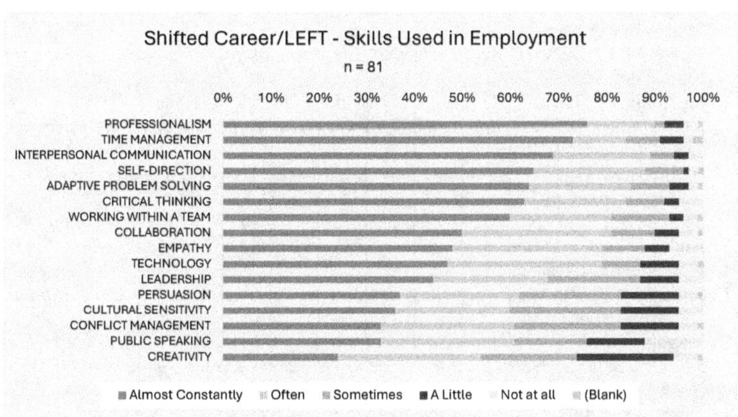

Figure 3.7 Skills used by Shifted Career/Left the Field participants in current employment.

indicated that, across all employment categories, transferable skills like these are present and in use as are less tangible skills like *confidence, active listening,* and *risk-taking.* Should a theatre graduate decide to shift fields and develop a career in another sector, the data makes clear that the skills developed during their undergraduate studies are likely to be an important part of that transition. A theatre degree does not provide all of the skills an employer may be seeking but it can provide an array of qualifications that apply to many fields. Because transferable skills are embedded in theatre training, college students in all fields would be well served to include some theatre training in their curriculum.

Notes

1 Gallup (Firm). (2019). *Forging pathways to purposeful work: The role of higher education.* Bates College.
2 Grossman, K. W. (2021, November 30). *What incentives are employers using to entice hourly workers? We have the scoop.* Talent Board. https://www.thetalentboard.org/article/what-incentives-are-employers-using-to-entice-hourly-workers-we-have-the-scoop/
3 Hart Research Associates. (2013, April 10). *It takes more than a major: Employer priorities for college learning and student success.* American Colleges and Universities/Hart Research Associates. https://www.aacu.org/sites/default/files/files/LEAP/2013_EmployerSurvey.pdf
4 Gallup (Firm). (2019). *Forging pathways to purposeful work: The role of higher education.* Bates College.
5 Molla, R., & Stewart, E. (2021, September 20). *Why everybody's hiring but nobody's getting hired. America's broken hiring system explained.* Voxmedia. https://www.vox.com/recode/22673353/unemployment-job-search-linkedin-indeed-algorithm
6 Weise, M. R. (2020). *Long life learning: Preparing for jobs that don't even exist yet.* John Wiley & Sons.
7 Weise, M. R. (2020). *Long life learning: Preparing for jobs that don't even exist yet.* John Wiley & Sons.
8 Sigelman, M., Taska, B., O'Kane, L., Nitschke, J., Strack, R., Baier, J., Breitling, F., & Kotsis, Á. (2022 May) *Shifting skills, moving targets, and remaking the workforce.* The Burning Glass Institute.
9 Blumenstyk, G. (2019). *Career-ready education: Beyond the skills gap, tools and tactics for an evolving economy.* Chronicle of Higher Education.
10 Scott, H. (2020, February 27). *Please stop calling them 'Soft Skills'.* Medium.
11 Anders, G. (2017). *You can do anything: The surprising power of a "useless" liberal arts education.* Hachette UK.
12 Silva, E. (2009). Measuring skills for 21st-century learning. *Phi Delta Kappan, 90*(9), 630–634.
13 Wagner, T. (2014). *The global achievement gap: Why even our best schools don't teach the new survival skills our children need—and what we can do about it.* Basic Books.
14 Oakley, K. (2007). *Educating for the creative workforce: Rethinking arts and education.* Australian Research Council Centre of Excellence for Creative Industries and Innovation.
15 Robles, M. (2012 December). Executive perceptions of the top 10 soft skills needed in today's workplace. *Business Communication Quarterly, 75*(4), 453–465.
16 Robles, M. (2012). Executive perceptions of the top 10 soft skills needed in today's workplace. *Business Communication Quarterly, 75*(4), 455.
17 Petrone, P. (2019, January 1). *The skills companies need most in 2019 – and how to learn them.* LinkedIn Corporation.
18 Trilling, B., & Fadel, C. (2009). *21st century skills: Learning for life in our times.* John Wiley & Sons.
19 Weise, M. R. (2020). *Long life learning: Preparing for jobs that don't even exist yet.* John Wiley & Sons.

20 Trilling, B., & Fadel, C. (2009). *21st century skills: Learning for life in our times.* John Wiley & Sons.
21 https://www.onetonline.org/link/localwages/27–2011.00?st=CO
22 Carnevale, A. P. (2013). *21st century competencies: For college and career readiness.* Center on Education and the Workforce.
23 https://aldacenter.org
24 Gagnon, S., Vough, H. C., & Nickerson, R. (2012). Learning to lead, unscripted: Developing affiliative leadership through improvisational theatre. *Human Resource Development Review, 11*(3), 299–325.
25 Hoffman, A., Utley, B., & Ciccarone, D. (2008). Improving medical student communication skills through improvisational theatre. *Medical Education, 42*(5), 537.
26 Ratten, V., & Hodge, J. (2016). So much theory, so little practice: A literature review of workplace improvisation training. *Industrial and Commercial Training, 48*(3), 149–155.
27 Kovacs, G. (2014). Applied drama and theatre–Drama techniques in teaching English for specific purposes. *Acta Universitatis Sapientiae, Philologica, 6*(3), 391–409.
28 Skaggs, R., Frenette, A., Gaskills, S., & Miller, A. (2017). Special report: Career skills and entrepreneurship training for artists – results of the 2015 SNAAP survey. *Strategic National Arts Alumni Project (SNAAP).* snaap.indiana.edu. Center for Postsecondary Research Indiana University School of Education.
29 https://www.indeed.com/q-Theatre-$50,000-l-USA-jobs.html?vjk=9a2d9b43170c29ee (accessed on April 21, 2024).
30 Of the 1,132 survey participants, 459 chose to contribute more information in the final open-ended survey question.

4 Value versus expense

Clare graduated five years ago with a major in theatre education. Her grades were strong, so she was able to gather a glowing collection of reference letters for her applications as a high school drama instructor. She landed a job right away in a district not far from her hometown. Her first year as a new teacher was challenging. She made many mistakes and struggled through some discouraging days, but eventually, she found her way. Clare learned quickly what was required to do her job, adapted her teaching process, and reinvented her curriculum. The students grew to love her and her classes in theatre study, and the high school productions she directed became popular on campus. Although Clare had found immediate employment in her chosen field upon graduation and now demonstrated exceptional competence at work, she was not happy. Even with a full-time job, her money was tight. She had borrowed $75,000 to complete her degree, money without which she would not have been able to attend college. Now that she was working, earning $48,000 per year, she was struggling to make ends meet. Her monthly take-home pay was just over $3,000. Her living expenses (rent, gas, food) were almost $2,000 per month, and her loan payment was $553, leaving her just under $500 for the unexpected. Clare had loved her college experience, and she was putting that investment into practice with employment in her chosen field. Five years into her employment journey, Clare had no regrets about getting a college degree in theatre. She just wondered how different her life might be if her college education had been more affordable.

The loss of public faith

According to a recent Gallup poll, the confidence of the American public in higher education has dropped to 36%, down from 48% in 2018.[1] The cost of tuition has risen sharply over the last several decades with many four-year degrees presenting a price tag of six figures. Some members of the public are concerned that the course content of an undergraduate degree may fail to provide skills that will lead to gainful employment.[2] Others fear that a university education may indoctrinate students with liberal ideas. Some are

DOI: 10.4324/9781003520023-5

questioning whether a college degree is even necessary anymore. Because the cost of a university education is so high, job placement following graduation has become even more critical. This puts pressure on academic leaders to support programs like business or healthcare as they offer a more reliable promise of future employment. It also leads them to question spending money on programs like philosophy, history, or theatre, courses of study that are less likely to generate employment in the field.[3] When students are required to dig deep to find the resources to pay for their education, they expect something exceptional in return. This Return on Investment paradigm has shifted the mission for many academic leaders from educating the whole student in service of the public good to concerns about enrollment revenues and customer satisfaction.[4] Challenges with a shrinking population, graduation rates, reductions in public funding, equity issues, and an outcry from the public about rising student debt have all contributed to a hard truth: the United States is no longer the most educated country in the world.[5] These, among many reasons, have led the public to question the value of a college degree as a ticket to economic independence.

The student as customer

Today, the student has become an education consumer, paying a premium price for a product they expect will return dividends in employability. They are now a customer[6] purchasing a commodity (their education) within a market-driven competitive environment, and for this pricey investment, they expect a high rate of return.[7] Students attend class to accrue credits toward a major they expect to serve as a ticket to employment in a specific field. Professors and students now engage in transactional activities with the payment of tuition representing a contract that must be fulfilled with reliable knowledge that results in immediate employment upon graduation.[8] Within such a paradigm, it can be challenging for administrators to advocate for the value of an arts degree. An arts degree often costs as much or more than any other degree but can only promise employment in the field for a minority of graduates and that only after several years of hard work establishing a professional portfolio. Administrators may not be aware of the crucial intangible benefits of an arts education, benefits that apply to students in every discipline and are precisely what the job market currently requires.[9]

Whether demonstrating immediate job placement or articulating the intangible benefits of college study, it has become clear that higher education must do a better job of communicating the value of a college degree if they hope to provide a positive future pathway for the students under their care. The Bill and Melinda Gates Foundation, concerned about the loss of public faith in higher education, commissioned the Postsecondary Value Report.[10] Their goal: to make a college education available to all who wish to study by providing more transparent and up-to-date information for prospective students, thereby allowing them to make an informed choice about their college investment.[11]

McMahon has argued for the importance of clearly communicating the value of university study for more than a decade. His concerns centered around institutional failure to identify and articulate the true market value of a college degree. In addition to offering future economic benefits, value definitions should include social benefits like better health, cognitive development, and personal happiness, elements that are less tangible but important components of an educational investment.[12] Lack of complete information could dissuade some from attending university, diminishing higher education's contribution to the public good. To increase efficiency and support informed decision-making, he recommended that all institutions create a one-page fact sheet that clearly articulates the full spectrum of the benefits provided by a college degree.

Earning potential as a decision-maker

A college degree can make a difference in the trajectory of a career. Even an unfinished degree can increase earning potential over a lifetime compared with an educational journey that ends with a high school diploma.[13] But college is not for everyone. One solution for those aspiring students who want more than a high school education but have little interest in college study is a vocational program. Vocational programs have become popular with conservative politicians. They appear void of the liberal politics attributed to many college campuses and are designed specifically for immediate employment upon graduation. Why your tax dollars should be spent to support degrees in philosophy or English literature is harder to demonstrate than support for certification as an airline mechanic or a computer repair technician. Some argue that vocational programs provide more employability and earning potential than many college degrees. While this may be true in the short term, lifetime earnings for a liberal arts degree will exceed the earning potential of most vocational training certificates.[14] In reality, employers have little interest in whether the applicant has a college degree or a vocational certificate. They want applicants to demonstrate the skills required to do the job. Where they get them is their business.[15]

Linking a college education to future earnings potential puts enormous pressure on graduating high school students. Whether they should attend college or vocational school, which institution, which major – all of these decisions seem enormously consequential for recent high school graduates. Given the cost of an education and the challenges the economy has been facing, they may believe that choosing poorly could tie them to a career path that pays them little or makes them unhappy in the long run.[16] Even though research indicates that a college graduate will change jobs several times over the course of their career, a prospective student might believe it is critically important to choose the right major and institution the first time, as many families will be unable to afford a do-over.[17] How to game this system can be challenging for students as they shop the market. Community colleges are the most affordable and private institutions are the most expensive. But research has indicated that, although a degree from a private not-for-profit university will cost more, those graduates will earn more over time than graduates from some public institutions.[18]

Tools like the College Scorecard, which gathers earning data from federal, state, and private sources[19] can help the decision-making process by providing detailed data on each institution.[20] According to the College Scorecard, as of October 10, 2023, if a student pursues a degree in mechanical engineering at the University of Arizona, they will accrue an average of $21,000 in debt with potential median earnings of just over $84,000. A degree in history at the same institution will set them back $22,500 but can only offer potential median earnings of $41,400. Using these figures, the decision seems clear – less debt and double the potential income – mechanical engineering it is. Unless, of course, the student has no interest in or aptitude for engineering. Employers have been complaining that graduates in fields like engineering lack the creative and interpersonal skills they need to function productively on the job. Christine Henseley argued that the history degree is more employable for the 21st-century job market given that it is unlikely that history majors will be employed in the field of history but will probably engage their education in any number of other fields.[21] In this debate – practical science versus frivolous humanities – George Anders agreed with Henseley arguing that liberal arts degrees offer the best pathway for future employment as they contain the greatest collection of adaptable skills.[22] Whether majoring in the arts, the humanities, engineering, or science, a combination of field specialization with a supplementary array of liberal arts classes at the undergraduate level offers the strongest resume in the current job market.[23]

The cost of an education

Whether an aspiring university student decides to major in business or women's studies, they will inevitably face one hard reality – the cost of their degree. The price tag for tuition, just one of a student's expenses during study, has been rising steadily over the past several decades, but has climbed significantly in the recent past. According to a report by Melanie Hansen in Education Data Initiative, a four-year undergraduate degree at a public university has increased 179.2% over the last 20 years.[24] There are several factors to blame for this astonishing statistic. A reduction in state funding has increased institutional reliance on tuition and student fees to make ends meet.[25] Increased demand has improved the market value for a college degree as applicants recognize the future monetary gain that may be achieved by a college education.

Table 4.1 National Averages as of December 29, 2023

Costs Per Year	*Four Years of Expenses*
Four year or above, public	$49,700
Four year or above, private, not for profit	$88,872
Four year or above, private, for profit	$93,452

Source: https://collegecost.ed.gov/affordability

Note: Average net price is generated by subtracting the average amount of federal, state/local government, or institutional grant or scholarship aid from the total cost of attendance. Total cost of attendance is the sum of published tuition and required fees (lower of in-district or in-state, where applicable), books and supplies, and the weighted average for room and board and other expenses. Average net price is for full-time beginning undergraduate students who received grant or scholarship aid from federal, state or local governments, or the institution. SOURCE: U.S. Department of Education, National Center for Education Statistics, Integrated Postsecondary Education Data System (IPEDS), Fall 2020, Institutional Characteristics component and Winter 2020–2021, Student Financial Aid component.

Finally, to attract students to their institutions, administrators have invested heavily in student services and administrative personnel (but not faculty positions). These outlays were intended to improve the student experience, but a recent report indicated that these expenditures have done nothing to increase graduation rates but have done much to increase the price tag for an education.[26] Table 4.1 identifies the average costs for students as of December 2023. If a student has between $50,000 and $100,000 to spend on a college degree, then future debt may not pose a problem if they choose their institution carefully. For many, student loans are the only option for a purchase of this magnitude.

Student loan debt has become a charged political issue with passionate positions on both sides of the loan forgiveness debate. The reality is that students who graduate with enormous debt must postpone important milestones like marriage, children, or the purchase of a first home.[27] Students in the United States pay significantly more than those in other countries like Canada or Japan where government subsidies help offset tuition expenses. In the European Union, some countries keep the price tag for college as close to zero as the economy will allow.[28] Students from those countries, should they choose to travel to the United States to study, will pay a tuition bill that is twice to three times as high as an American student for the same education.[29] This conundrum, that a degree promises more future monetary gain but to acquire that degree one must shoulder significant financial debt, is particularly challenging for aspiring artists. The process of starting an artistic career requires a flexible and non-demanding employment situation, one where the artist may pick up or drop non-arts employment at will when an artistic opportunity presents itself. The responsibility for large monthly payments on student debt makes this paradigm challenging to achieve. More student debt results in a lower likelihood that the arts graduate will have an opportunity to establish a professional career following graduation.[30]

The neoliberal paradigm

Profit-based decision-making has invaded higher education. University administrators have been pressured by governing boards and state politicians to carefully examine tuition-based revenue streams as a method of determining which programs are appropriate to keep on campus and which are no longer of value to the institution. The logic goes that if a large number of students are drawn to study business or engineering, we should continue to offer and possibly increase the number of spots available in business and engineering programs. If fewer students are studying history, philosophy, or the visual arts, that is an indication that these programs are no longer important to the job market and therefore of little value. This supply and demand framework has a Darwinian component – those programs that can demonstrate sufficient enrollment will survive. Those that cannot will be eliminated. The consumer (the student) will signal through enrollment which educational choices are important to the employment marketplace, even though that consumer may have no idea what precisely they want in a career nor how best to go about meeting that goal. The real consequence of using this paradigm to determine the programs available on campus is that the training provided by the arts and humanities is exactly what the marketplace is seeking – critical thinking about complicated disciplinary intersections presented within an environment that encourages conversation, dissent, and the ability to defend one's point of view in written form.[31]

Neoliberalism is a loaded term within the academy. Defining it precisely can be challenging. It is understood to be a philosophy that wishes to deregulate capital markets,[32] "favors private enterprise and seeks to transfer the control of economic factors for the government to the private sector,"[33] and claims as its primary value "free market competition."[34] For higher education, this translates to a framework that encourages activities that make money and discourages those that do not. It also suggests that government funding for an enterprise that is not profitable would be ill-advised, as public funding should not be used to "prop up" activities that should thrive on their own or disappear. When politicians and decision-makers adopt such a position, they can change the climate and curriculum of an institution. Programs that generate high enrollments and strong graduation rates become more valuable than those with smaller enrollments as enrollments equate directly to tuition dollars. Within this framework, the quality of learning is secondary, and the revenue earned is primary.[35] Neoliberal mindsets can change which majors are offered, the number of students per classroom, and the number of classes an instructor teaches per term. Funneling the maximum number of students through the system is prioritized over learning outcomes. An instructor leading a classroom of 400 students will teach differently from an instructor with a room of 20. In a lecture hall of 400, there may be little time to engage in critical discourse or challenging conversations over the course of a semester. Within a neoliberal context, whether the student can retain and apply the information they learned in this classroom is of secondary importance. More valuable is the fact that 400 students per instructor are more cost-effective than 20. Under these conditions, it seems a liberal arts degree would hardly stand a chance. Many of the classes in a liberal arts classroom are smaller, often ranging from 16 to 40 students, and the subject matter may appear esoteric or irrelevant to the skills required for today's employment market. After all, what value can a seminar on medieval poetry or Asian history provide in a world that is struggling with the impacts of technology and regional conflicts across the globe? A student's time and money would be better spent learning supply chain management or applied linear algebra even if they have no interest in those subjects. This paradigm, processing as many students as possible within a four-to-six-year time frame and then dropping them into a complicated and dynamic job market is part of why employers are frustrated. It takes time and money to nurture and develop critical thinkers and creative problem solvers, and many institutions are struggling to afford such luxuries.

The challenge of performance indicators

The slow creep toward a neoliberal mindset in higher education is putting academic leaders in a bind. As cuts in government funding reduce revenues and personnel costs increase to cover new student services something must give.[36] Administrators are under enormous pressure to prove value for dollars spent and hold themselves accountable for the employability of the degrees they confer on students who often go into debt to acquire them. When their budgets must be balanced, one of the first places academic leaders turn is program reduction.[37] But how is an administrator to choose which programs should stay and which should go? Every department on campus will certainly argue passionately for saving their programs. Some administrators have begun to adopt a rating system as a way of objectively identifying the value of specific courses of study.[38] These quantitative assessment tools, often referred to as performance indicators, are intended to fairly evaluate all programs across the institution using measurements such as alignment with the university's mission, cost of delivery, number of students reaching completion, and employment within two years of the degree. Most of these metrics are based on economic values – cost for delivery versus tuition revenue, ability to attract donors, contributions to institutional reputation – values that work in favor of programs such as business and engineering but disfavor almost all of those in the arts and humanities.[39] The use of performance indicators is sometimes justified as a method to demonstrate value to taxpayers, although compared to other countries the American taxpayer is contributing less and less to higher education as states continue to cut their contributions to these institutions.[40]

The reality of program cuts

Budget cuts, the elimination of programs and faculty positions, and a reliance on performance indicators that favor some degrees over others – all of these trends are a threat to arts and humanities programs. Because the research has made clear that these programs are providing the training that is currently at a deficit among recent graduates, it is important to find compelling evidence that could persuade academic leaders to calculate return on investment using metrics that transcend traditional economic drivers. Should university presidents continue to eliminate arts programs, they may be removing foundational components of an educational experience that help shape our future leaders.[41]

Budgets at universities have become increasingly tight. As demographics shift, there are fewer and fewer students available to enroll at many institutions, reducing one of higher education's most important revenue streams. Some predict that college enrollment will experience an even sharper decline in the next few years, exacerbating concerns about the drop in tuition revenue.[42] Given the current fiscal crisis, administrators have felt enormous pressure to take some action, even with limited data, and performance indicators provide at least one way to decide on program cuts.[43] There is a growing increase in the number of university presidents who are looking to cut academic programs to save money.[44] When these programs are cut, the faculty who oversee them may also disappear.[45] Even institutions in Canada have become worried that their humanities and fine arts programs may not survive this growing trend.[46]

This fear became a reality for the University of Wisconsin Superior in 2017 when the administration announced that they were cutting 24 programs, including majors in theatre and art history. The president insisted that the cuts were motivated by a need to protect first-generation students who were overwhelmed by the number of programs on offer, and he promised that program reductions would increase the graduation rates for this demographic. Given the patronizing content of this justification and the reality of the 2.5-billion-dollar deficit the university was facing, the faculty chose to disbelieve the president's rationale and pushed back complaining that they had not been consulted on this important institutional decision.[47] The University of Wisconsin Stevens Point experienced a similar crisis. In March of 2018, cuts to 13 programs were reduced to six after much protest by students, faculty, and alumni, although plans remained to add 16 vocational programs to their roster.[48] These were not isolated incidents. Table 4.2 identifies only some of the most recent cuts to university programs.

Table 4.2 Cuts to Programs Since 2017

What Was Cut	*Dates of Cuts*	*Institution*
135 programs, including philosophy, music, and **theatre**.	August 2017	Morningside College
15 programs, including philosophy, political science, sociology, and museum studies.	October 2019	University of St. Francis
Philosophy, religion, **theatre**, dance, musical performance, and languages and graduate programs in art, fine arts, education, history, anthropology, mathematics, physics, chemistry, biochemistry, geophysics, and geosciences.	November 2019	University of Tulsa
Departments of sociology and t**heatre**	February 2020	University of Alaska Anchorage
18 majors, including journalism	October 2020	Ohio Wesleyan University
Programs in education	October 2020	University of South Florida
Drama, theatre and performance, and dance	November 2020	University of Roehampton (UK)
12 majors, including classical civilization, geology, German, Greek, Asian studies, Latin American and Caribbean studies, Italian studies, Latin and religion	December 2020	University of Vermont
Cut the music department and then changed their mind	February 2021	University of Evansville
Closing all programs – graduate and undergraduate and becoming an institute	March 2021	Mills College
34 programs in English and 24 programs in French	April 2021	Laurentian University
Majors in German and Nordic studies; minors in classical studies, German and Norwegian	April 2021	Pacific Lutheran
Closed the dance program	September 2021	University of Arkansas at Little Rock
Intake pause for 16 programs, including European Studies, **arts** history, and nine science programs.	May 2023	University of Guelph
338 majors, consolidating several programs.	August 2023	West Virginia University
Eight programs, including English, history, philosophy, and **theatre**.	October 2023	Newman University
Nine programs, including **theatre**, musical theatre, and geography.	November 2023	University of Nebraska Kearney
15 programs, including international studies and business law.	December 2023	Bradley University

Politicians and the academy

The political pressure academic leaders are currently experiencing cannot be understated. Jeff Selingo found this a good thing as he articulated that higher education is overdue for major change.[49] When conservative politicians are asked why they are so unhappy with higher education, many of them indicate a concern about ideology. They believe universities are too liberally inclined and that most classes are taught by professors who share these views. This situation reached a crisis point in December 2023 with the congressional testimonies of three presidents of prestigious universities.[50] The perceived failure of these institutional leaders to appropriately answer questions on antisemitism created a fervor in conservative circles, with Republicans in the House using this moment to call for investigations into accreditation and offering proposals to ban public funding for some institutions.[51]

Cutting public funding and advocating for more vocational schools is an argument that works well for politicians as tuition and cost of living expenses continue to climb.[52] They can comfortably advocate for supporting degrees that demonstrate clear employability upon graduation. This is great news for vocational programs as there is currently a shortage of blue-collar workers in the United States.[53] Arts degrees are unlikely to appeal to someone interested in a tight fiscal budget. Arts degrees are frivolous, do not contribute to the economy (so they say, although research says otherwise, even in conservative states like Florida),[54] encourage radical thinking, and arts graduates are likely to be unemployed and in debt once they have graduated. Debt and unemployment are indeed likely outcomes for arts graduates in the first few years following graduation, but as these graduates establish careers, the adaptability of their degrees provides the potential for them to earn much more over a lifetime than graduates of vocational programs.

What the survey told us

A college degree should lead to gainful employment. We have seen that the field in which a college graduate will work may change several times over the course of their career and that it is not uncommon for graduates to work in a field other than their major. The majority of theatre graduates in this study (69%) found work in other fields, and most of them used the skills acquired with their degree in this work. Given this information, I wanted to better understand if participants in the study were happy with their current employment.

When participants were asked if they were content with their current employment, they indicated that, for the most part, they were. A plurality selected moderate satisfaction at 46% followed by high satisfaction at 41% for a total of 87% of at least moderate satisfaction. Participants also offered several insights regarding these levels of satisfaction. Having to work multiple jobs was of concern for some, "I put somewhat dissatisfied with my current employment because I have had to work multiple day jobs since graduating with my theatre degree" [*Moderately unsatisfied*]; while other respondents were more neutral about this circumstance, "I spent a lot of years doing different kinds of work, entrepreneurial and otherwise, to support my artistic habits" [*Moderately satisfied*].

A few participants were clear about their frustrations regarding underemployment, "a lot of people get paid to work professionally but it's not enough money to live on independently" [*Moderately unsatisfied*]. Others, who also acknowledged underemployment had no regrets, "the technology I learned allowed me to get a much higher-paying job in an industrial design field, but I was again unhappy leaving theatre and eventually took a pay cut to return" [*Very satisfied*].

Some participants wanted to communicate the complexity of their employment situation, "While only 5% of my work life (i.e., paychecks) are from theatre, I use skills I learned in my 95% day job every single day" [*Moderately satisfied*]. Others wanted to convey that the theatre system contains inequities that informed their situation. This included sexism: "Women are extremely underrepresented backstage" [*Very satisfied*]; racism: "I'm Black. Fewer jobs available" [*Moderately satisfied*]; and ableism: "My program was very ableist, that is why I am no longer pursuing acting" [*Very satisfied*] (Figure 4.1).

Given the levels of satisfaction with their career trajectories, I wanted to know if participants would choose to major in theatre again if given the chance. Hindsight often provides a useful perspective and the certainty one may hold about future career prospects at the age of 18 may shift with time. In Chapter 2, we learned that theatre majors often chose the degree intending to work in the field of theatre upon graduation. Knowing what they knew now about the reality of their career path and the expense of the degree, I wondered if they would make the same decision again. 64% of participants indicated that they would definitely major in theatre again, with another 25% stating that they might major again if given the chance. This total (89%) was in alignment with levels of employment satisfaction (87%) suggesting a link between the degree and employment happiness. The question regarding a willingness to major again helped amplify the transferability of a theatre education to other fields as the majority of these graduates were currently working part-time or full-time outside of the field of theatre (Figure 4.2).

The price tag for a theatre degree varied considerably for participants in the study. Some attended state universities with a lower tuition obligation, others studied in the Ivy League. Financial resources were variable as well. Some students studied on scholarship or through the grace of parents who could afford to pay their tuition. Others had to save and work throughout their degree and may have graduated with substantial student debt. The cost of studying theatre and having the resources available for university study had the potential to impact participants' perception of the value of their degree. When I asked participants

Satisfaction with Current Employment
n = 1132

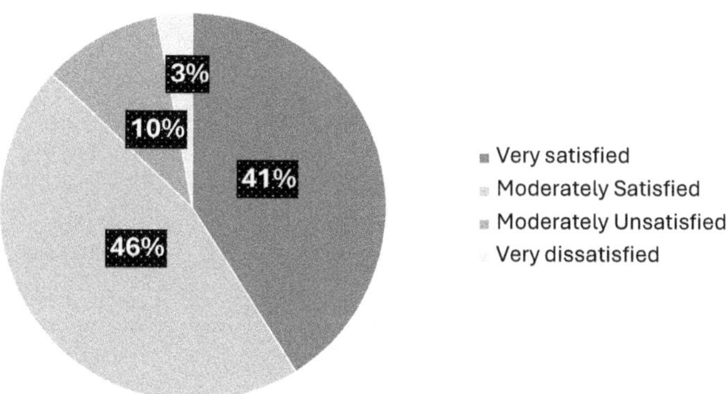

Figure 4.1 Participants' satisfaction levels with current employment.

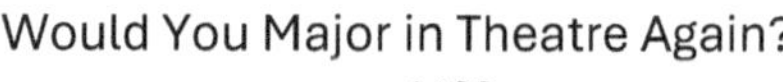

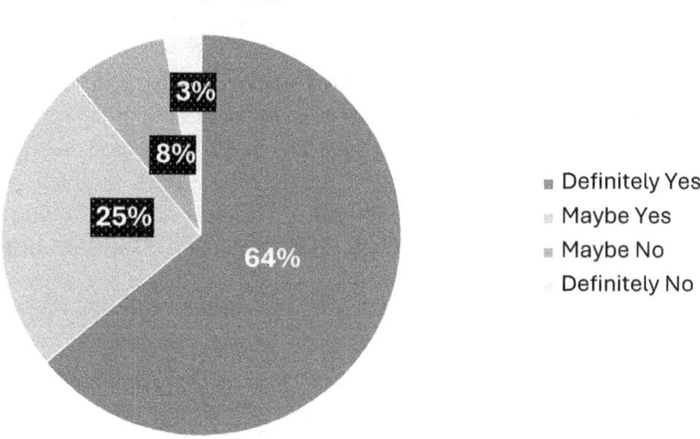

Figure 4.2 Levels of willingness to major in theatre again.

whether their degree was worth the money spent, 50% indicated definitely yes and an additional 34% selecting maybe yes for a total of 84%. Again, this aligned with employment satisfaction (87%) and interest in majoring in theatre again (89%). The evidence from the survey identified that participants found value in their degree through satisfying employment, that given what they know now they would major in theatre again, and that they believed their degree to have been worth the money spent (Figure 4.3).

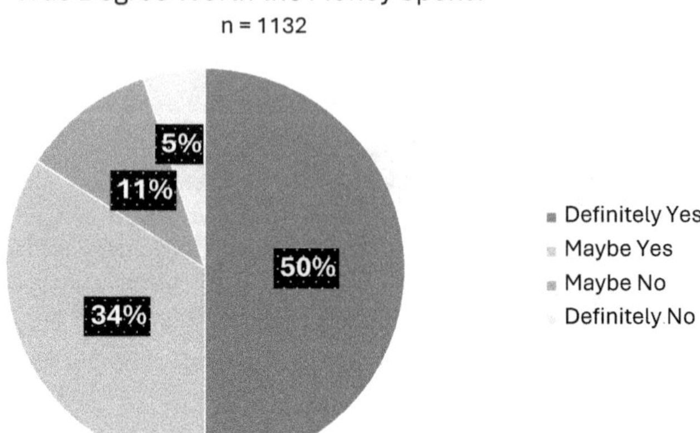

Figure 4.3 Determining whether the degree was worth the money spent.

In summary

The participants in this study identified important factors regarding the perceived value of their theatre degree. The majority were satisfied with their current employment, held an interest in majoring in theatre again, and believed that their theatre degree was worth the money spent to acquire it. Because a college degree is one of the most expensive purchases a person will make, students, parents, university administrators, and the general public expect that any course of study will lead to a job in that field. Those majoring in subjects like business, engineering, or medicine anticipate that the skills acquired with their degree will qualify them for employment. Although this may be true, employers have begun to complain that skills like interpersonal communication, teamwork, critical thinking, and creative problem solving are missing in the skill sets of many college graduates. To meet employer expectations in this dynamic and evolving contemporary job market, students would be well served to supplement their primary degree with a collection of transferable skills from a program like theatre.

The realities faced by university administrators today are grim: declining enrollments due to demographic shifts are reducing revenue, attacks from conservative politicians are diminishing government support, and the public is demanding accountability regarding the astronomical increase in the cost of a college degree. To restore the public's faith in the value of this investment, academic leaders are scrambling to provide evidence that the money spent on a college education will result in a good job. The metrics administrators are currently using to identify programs to eliminate from their budgets comprise an existential threat to arts programs like theatre. Theatre classes enroll a smaller number of students, few theatre graduates will find work in the field immediately upon graduation, and theatre programs require substantial institutional support to function. All of these factors work against demonstrating the value of a degree in theatre, but eliminating programs like theatre will remove important learning opportunities that contribute directly to the employability of all students on campus. In addition, the participants in this study have demonstrated that not only does a theatre degree lead to employment, but it can qualify a graduate for employment in a wide variety of fields with a strong probability of job satisfaction.

Notes

1 Brenan, M. (2023). *Americans' confidence in education down sharply.* Gallup, Inc. https://news.gallup.com/poll/508352/americans-confidence-higher-education-down-sharply.aspx
2 Blumenstyk, G. (2019). The innovation imperative: The buzz, the barriers, and what real change looks like. *The Chronicle of Higher Education.*
3 Tough, P. (2023, September 5). *Americans are losing faith in the value of college. Whose fault is that?* NY Times Magazine. https://www.nytimes.com/2023/09/05/magazine/college-worth-price.html
4 Carlson, S. (2019). The right mix of academic programs: Making decisions to add, cut, grow, or shrink departments and degrees. *The Chronicle of Higher Education.*
5 World Population Review. (2024). https://worldpopulationreview.com/country-rankings/most-educated-countries
6 Stokes, P. J. (2017). *Higher education and employability: New models for integrating study and work.* Harvard Education Press.
7 Stokes, P. J. (2017). *Higher education and employability: New models for integrating study and work.* Harvard Education Press.
8 Kaye, T., Bickel, R. R., & Birtwistle, T. (2006). Criticizing the image of the student as consumer: Examining legal trends and administrative responses in the US and UK. *Education and the Law, 18*(2–3), 85–129.
9 Bowen, D. H., & Kisida, B. (2019). Investigating causal effects of arts education experiences: Experimental evidence from Houston's arts access initiative. *Research Report for the Houston Independent School District. 7*(4). Houston Education Research Consortium.
10 Institution for Higher Education Policy & The Bill and Melinda Gates Foundation. (2021). *Equitable value: Promoting economic mobility and social justice through postsecondary education.* Postsecondary Value Commission.
11 Jaschik, S. (2021, May 12). *Redefining 'value' in higher education.* Inside Higher Ed. https://www.educationaladvisors.com/redefining-value-in-higher-education/
12 McMahon, W. W. (2009). *Higher learning, greater good: The private and social benefits of higher education.* Johns Hopkins University Press.
13 Carnevale, A. P., Rose, S. J., & Cheah, B. (2011). *The college payoff: Education, occupations, lifetime earnings.* Center on Education and the Workforce, Georgetown University.
14 Humphreys, D., & Kelly, P. (2014). How liberal arts and sciences majors fare in employment: A report on earnings and long-term career paths. *Peer Review, 16*(2), 31–32.
15 Comunian, R., Faggian, A., & Jewell, S. (2011). Winning and losing in the creative industries: An analysis of creative graduates' career opportunities across creative disciplines. *Cultural Trends, 20*(3–4), 291–308.

16 Selingo, J. J. (2013). *College (un) bound: The future of higher education and what it means for students.* Houghton Mifflin Harcourt.
17 Cappelli, P. (2015). *Will college pay off? A guide to the most important financial decision you'll ever make.* PublicAffairs.
18 Seltzer, R. (2019, November 14). *Return on students' investments varies over time.* Inside Higher Ed. https://www.insidehighered.com/news/2019/11/14/differences-college-roi-vary-institution-type-and-time-frame-measured-report-says#:~:text=An%20average%20private%20college%20graduate,years%20after%20enrollment%20was%20%24107%2C000.
19 The College Scorecard gathers earnings information from federal student loan data, state tax records, Payscale, and comparisons with the Census Bureau's Post-Secondary Employment Outcomes.
20 https://collegescorecard.ed.gov
21 Henseler, C. (2017, August 18). *Liberal arts is the foundation for professional success in the 21st century.* ET Huffington Post.
22 Anders, G. (2017). *You can do anything: The surprising power of a "useless" liberal arts education.* Hachette UK.
23 Wildavsky, B. (2023, August 21). *Let's stop pretending college degrees don't matter.* NY Times. https://www.nytimes.com/2023/08/21/opinion/skills-based-hiring-college-degree-job-market-wage-premium.html
24 Hanson, M. (2022, January 9). *Average cost of college by year.* EducationData.org. https://educationdata.org/average-cost-of-college-by-year
25 Newfield, C. (2018). *The great mistake: How we wrecked public universities and how we can fix them.* Johns Hopkins University Press.
26 American Council of Trustees and Alumni. (2021). *The cost of excess: Why colleges and universities must control runaway spending.* American Council of Trustees and Alumni.
27 Selingo, J. J. (2013). *College (un) bound: The future of higher education and what it means for students.* Houghton Mifflin Harcourt.
28 Tough, P. (2023, September 5). *Americans are losing faith in the value of college. Whose fault is that?* NY Times Magazine. https://www.nytimes.com/2023/09/05/magazine/college-worth-price.html
29 https://www.idp.com/middleeast/study-in-usa/cost-of-study/?lang=en
30 Lindemann, D. J., & Tepper, S. J. (2012). *Painting with broader strokes: Reassessing the value of an arts degree--based on the results of the 2010 Strategic National Arts Alumni Project. Special Report 1.* Strategic National Arts Alumni Project.
31 Svrluga, S. (2020, January 13). *Liberal arts education: Waste of money or practical investment? Study's conclusions might surprise you.* The Washington Post.
32 https://en.wikipedia.org/wiki/Neoliberalism#cite_note-FOOTNOTEBoasGans-Morse2009-7
33 Manning, M. (2022, July 29). *Neoliberalism: What it is, with examples and pros and cons.* Investopedia. https://www.investopedia.com/terms/n/neoliberalism.asp
34 https://www.britannica.com/money/topic/neoliberalism
35 Grassian, D. (2015). The new U: Higher education in the 21st century. *American Jewish University. Journal of Higher Education Management, 30*(1), 216–232.
36 Breaking the trade-off between cost and quality: Sustaining mission in an era of constrained resources. (2019). *Education Advisory Board.* https://eab.com/research/academic-affairs/on-demand-webconference/breaking-the-trade-off-between-cost-and-quality/
37 Carlson, S. (2019). The right mix of academic programs: Making decisions to add, cut, grow, or shrink departments and degrees. *The Chronicle of Higher Education.*
38 Davis, O. (2013, October 9). *6 ways neoliberal education reform is destroying our college system.* Alternet. https://www.salon.com/2013/10/09/6_ways_neoliberal_education_reform_is_destroying_our_college_system_partner/

39 Carlson, S. (2019). The right mix of academic programs: Making decisions to add, cut, grow, or shrink departments and degrees. *The Chronicle of Higher Education.*

40 Itzkowitz, M. (2020, April 1). *Price-to-earnings premium: A new way of measuring return on investment in higher ed.* Third Way. https://www.thirdway.org/report/price-to-earnings-premium-a-new-way-of-measuring-return-on-investment-in-higher-ed

41 Henseler, C. (2017, August 18). Liberal arts is the foundation for professional success in the 21st century. *ET Huffington Post.*

42 Conley, B. (2019, September 6). *The great enrollment crash: Students aren't showing up and it's only going to get worse.* The Chronicle of Higher Education. https://www.chronicle.com/article/the-great-enrollment-crash/?sra=true.

43 Hubler, S. (2020, October 26). *Colleges slash budgets in the pandemic, with 'nothing off-limits.'* New York Times. https://www.nytimes.com/2020/10/26/us/colleges-coronavirus-budget-cuts.html

44 Lederman, D. (2020, June 29). *Presidents' growing worry? Perceived value of college.* Inside Higher Ed. https://silverfernadvisory.com/strategy-tips/f/presidents-growing-worry-perceived-value-of-college

45 Chronicle staff. (2020, July 2). *As Covid-19 pummels budgets, colleges are resorting to layoffs and furloughs. Here's the latest.* Chronicle of Higher Education. https://www.chronicle.com/article/were-tracking-employees-laid-off-or-furloughed-by-colleges/

46 Peters, D. (2021, February 22). *Performance-based funding comes to the Canadian postsecondary sector: Ontario unveils its new funding formula for colleges and universities as Alberta mulls its own PBF scheme.* University Affairs. https://www.universityaffairs.ca/news/news-article/performance-based-funding-comes-to-the-canadian-postsecondary-sector/

47 Mangan, K. (2017, November 1). *Plan to phase out 2 dozen programs stuns faculty at Wisconsin-Superior.* Chronicle of Higher Education. https://www.chronicle.com/article/plan-to-phase-out-2-dozen-programs-stuns-faculty-at-wisconsin-superior/

48 Crowe, C. (2018, November 12). *How one university went from proposing to cut 13 mostly liberal- arts programs to eliminating only 6.* Chronicle of Higher Education. https://www.chronicle.com/article/how-one-university-went-from-proposing-to-cut-13-mostly-liberal-arts-programs-to-eliminating-only-6/

49 Selingo, J. J. (2013). *College (un) bound: The future of higher education and what it means for students.* Houghton Mifflin Harcourt.

50 Ma, A. (2023, December 12). How the presidents of Harvard, Penn, and MIT testified to congress on antisemitism. *The Associated Press.* https://apnews.com/article/harvard-penn-mit-president-congress-intifada-193a1c81e9ebcc15c5dd68b71b4c6b71#

51 Karni, A. (2024, January 5). *House republicans to broaden higher education inquiry beyond antisemitism.* NY Times. https://www.nytimes.com/2024/01/05/us/politics/house-republicans-antisemitism-colleges-harvard.html

52 Tough, P. (2023, September 5). *Americans are losing faith in the value of college. Whose fault is that?* NY Times Magazine. https://www.nytimes.com/2023/09/05/magazine/college-worth-price.html

53 Wilkie, D. (2019, February 2). *The blue collar drought.* SHRM. https://www.shrm.org/topics-tools/news/all-things-work/blue-collar-drought

54 https://dos.fl.gov/cultural/info-and-opportunities/resources-by-topic/economic-impact-of-the-arts/#:~:text=The%20arts%20are%20a%20vitally,impact%20studies%20to%20national%20reports.

5 Changing the message

A theatre education has much to offer students who are seeking to become more employable in today's economy. Theatre educators, theatre artists, and the students who learn from them would be well served to find a way to communicate this value to members of other disciplines and the general public. Multiple obstacles stand in the way of this goal: perception bias (theatre study is frivolous), reluctance to engage in new practices (change is frightening), and a lack of data supporting the claim that a theatre degree teaches skills that may be applied to many fields.

The academy must adapt

The challenge for educators who develop and deliver curricular programs is to anticipate which skills will be required for employment post-graduation. We can only guess at what will be required and offer students an education that is creative and adaptable with learning outcomes that are responsive to the needs of jobs that do not yet exist.[1] It is possible to imagine that for some fields, the skills a student will need for employment when entering a degree may have changed significantly by the time they graduate (think any field that depends heavily on technology). This does not obviate the value of the education a student has received, but it does require academics to rethink how to make graduates more employable.

Employers have made their position clear. They are less interested in pedigrees and more interested in skills and talent.[2] Derrick Rancourt argued that we should be training "versitalists" rather than specialists.[3] We must educate students with core skill sets, but most of all, we must train them to be flexible, open, and adaptable in a dynamic employment marketplace. The rising prevalence of artificial intelligence in all fields offers the promise that some jobs formerly performed by humans will disappear. We have been here before – the industrial revolution, the invention of the automobile, robots in factories, computers, the internet – there always seems to be some innovation that disrupts the labor market. The only difference between now and then is the speed of change. It may not be possible for a university education to

DOI: 10.4324/9781003520023-6

keep pace with changes in technology, medicine, or manufacturing, but arts training is well-equipped to offer the adaptable skills that fields like computer science and engineering do not.

The challenges we face

To provide a relevant and rich educational experience in the 21st century, we will need adaptive curricular strategies and a more responsive understanding of what employers are seeking. Career preparation for entry into the job market can no longer function as an afterthought during the final year of study. Strategies for an adaptable career should be embedded throughout an undergraduate education.[4] We need to begin to think outside of our disciplinary traditions and consider new modes of engagement, identifying those segments of learning that are essential to specialization as well as those that might be applied across sectors.[5]

Contemporary universities have inherited an educational tradition that is over 1,000 years old.[6] Tradition is and always has been important to the academy. Even from the time of ancient Greece, a university education was understood to function as a pathway to employment. Theatre departments and their respective curriculums emerged in response to a growing theatre industry and the need for trained professionals. Such a paradigm no longer exists and the number of theatres offering employment to young graduates is shrinking. As the data in this study made clear, we are currently training the majority of our students for probable unemployment in the theatre industry (although gainful employment in other industries). This presents an existential threat to our field of study. To justify the resources spent to continue including theatre programs in the academy, we must overcome our need to adhere closely to traditional theatre training and begin to rethink our purpose. We have the tools to make ourselves essential to the job market through the array of transferable skills that are a natural component of our curriculum if only we are willing to reconsider how we frame our position.

What an arts degree already offers

In a universe of tight budgets and competing agendas, it can be challenging to argue for the value of a theatre degree. Javier Cevallos recommended that, rather than resisting the pressure to justify majors in the arts, we should identify what makes artists unique and sell those qualities to the prospective college student.[7] John Freeman supported this idea. He argued that as economies become more reliant on the transferable skills available through an arts degree, educators should train students to consider pathways toward employment that include arts study. He called this paradigm "informed uncertainty" and argued that it equips graduates with the skills they need to respond to a dynamic and evolving economy.[8]

Some educators have advocated for more applied learning in an undergraduate degree to address the need for transferable skills. Tech industry leaders, frustrated by a lack of productivity and innovation in their companies, are calling for training in emotional intelligence, conflict management, communication, self-awareness, and problem-solving in teams.[9] Interest in these human/soft/transferable skills has evolved into a new educational movement known as SHAPE. Formerly, the promotion of study in STEM fields (science, technology, engineering, and math) was considered the answer to the skills deficits of contemporary education. STEM's failure to provide everything employers needed became the STEAM movement (adding arts to the acronym). Today we have a more robust call for the inclusion of arts and humanities in SHAPE (social sciences, humanities, the arts for people and the economy).[10] Considered a "re-brand" by the British Academy, the Arts Council, and the London School of Economics, there is hope that SHAPE can help amplify the value of "softer" subjects for students in all disciplines.[11]

Employers could not be clearer about the skills they want from applicants. When asked by the Chronicle of Higher Education how important soft skills were to the current job market, 81% of employers answered *Very Important*, particularly following the crisis of the pandemic.[12] Arts departments like theatre have transferable skills training embedded in their curriculum. Theatre educators are already preparing students for adaptable employment. Now we must make our graduates aware of the marketability of their theatre skills and the application of these skills to many possible career paths as well as sharing this important training with students in other disciplines.

Expanding our curriculum

Many arts graduates have expressed satisfaction with the education they received during their college degree. They have also signaled the need for more help transitioning from the college campus to the professional world. This transition gap is an opportunity for educators to help graduates understand how what they have learned with an arts degree may be applied to multiple employment paradigms.[13] Matthews identified the process of helping creative graduates make the shift from the academy to the world of work as one of *translation* rather than transition.[14] Helping students recognize how the skills they have acquired may be translated to multiple fields broadens their opportunities for creative work. Ferguson recommended shifting the question for graduates from "What will I become?" to "How can I make a difference?"[15] a perspective that could help bolster an arts graduate's sense of purpose as they work through the early years of career development.

Research has demonstrated that most arts graduates will shift fields at some point in their careers. Without proper context, these graduates may identify a career shift as a failure, even though shifting careers has become the norm in many fields.[16] Arts educators can address the professional transition gap by flipping the script, making explicit the value of the skills their students have acquired during their arts studies and the possible ways these skills might enhance future employment. Through such efforts, educators can increase a graduate's self-confidence as they enter the job market, broaden the number of career possibilities for them, and transform the perception of failure to one of opportunity for those who choose to pursue a career outside of the arts.

Participants in this study shared what they appreciated about their theatre education and identified some areas as deficits. Business skills appeared several times as one of the missing topics. These graduates felt ill-prepared to understand the financial implications of embarking on a career in the theatre. The 2022 Campus Skills Report suggested that all university graduates need some fundamental business training as a part of their curriculum.[17] Business skills are important for an arts graduate as those who continue to pursue an arts career will become self-employed for at least some period of time. The business skills required for self-employment may be of particular value to a theatre student. Theatre artists must analyze the market in which they hope to work, identify potential sources of employment, put together a sales package (headshots, resumes, portfolios), and then engage in the long and often grueling process of selling themselves as their product. Theatre students would benefit from classes that cover budgeting, sales and marketing, strategic planning, contract negotiation, legal issues, and filling out tax forms.[18] All of these skills could contribute to their potential future careers as artists and would apply to many other fields as well.[19]

The second important topic missing in some theatre degrees is an intentional focus on digital literacy. Digital skills have emerged as a requirement for nearly every profession and every field, including the arts, and almost all disciplines now include some form of technology training. A combination of digital "hard" skills and a collection of transferable "soft" skills appear to address the greatest employment gap at present.[20] What constitutes digital literacy appears to be changing and evolving at the current pace of technology requiring adaptability and a willingness to engage in a career-long learning process. In the early 2000s, the concept of the digital native was prevalent in many educational conversations. A digital native was understood as a person who had access to and/or engaged with some form of technology throughout their lifetime. That is, they had never known a world without a computer of some sort.[21] Access to technology has impacted everyone born after 1980 and shaped the way they learn. According to Charles Kivunja, changes in learning behavior for digital natives include a need for freedom of choice, agency in decision-making, an interest in customizing the learning experience, more of a tendency to collaborate than their generational predecessors, a tendency toward suspicion and scrutiny of organizations, a tendency to rely on the internet to acquire new information, a need for speed, love of innovation, an interest in fun, and a hunger for opportunities to create.[22]

Given the ways technology has impacted and shaped digital natives, one might assume they come by digital literacy naturally. But true digital literacy constitutes more than the ability to turn on and use a computer or a smartphone. Digital literacy requires the ability to access information, understand it, analyze its relevance, and then determine a course of action situated within an ethical context.[23] A study seeking to identify a list of 21st-century digital skills produced the following: technical ability (operating the machine), information management (accessing and manipulating data), communication (engaging with others via various platforms), collaboration (using platforms for teamwork), creativity (using technology to generate new ideas), critical thinking (assessing and judging the information acquired), problem-solving (determining actions to take), ethical-awareness (recognizing the potential impact of the actions taken), self-direction (the ability to work independently), and life-long learning (recognizing that understanding technology requires an ongoing interest in learning something new).[24] Although there is an overlap of these skills with some of the transferable skills acquired with a theatre degree, it is worth considering how theatre educators might amplify those skills by including more digital literacy in a theatre curriculum.

Some elements of contemporary theatre training already include technology. Design classes can teach students to render, plot, generate elevations, and ground plans on a computer rather than with pencil and paper. Most lighting boards are programmable and lighting instruments continue to evolve offering more aesthetic (and programming) possibilities. Sound and projection design share many of these characteristics. Even a set model could be generated via 3-D printing. But what about digital literacy training in areas like acting, dramaturgy, playwriting, or directing? Computers are regularly used for research and writing in many subjects, but are there other ways in which we might incorporate digital literacy in these classes? And how does the use of social media figure into our curriculum? It is an important part of marketing plans for the business sector and offers ample opportunity for critical thinking and ethics studies.

The pandemic lockdown forced academics to engage digital platforms to accommodate online teaching and learning, resulting in the use of educational software like Jamboard and Moodle. Other tools like Slack and Grammarly are now commonly used by many educators.[25] The number of online teaching tools continues to proliferate offering opportunities for theatre educators to supplement in-person learning with digital engagement. Teaching centers at many universities have become deeply involved in studying how artificial intelligence will impact learning. Theatre educators need to include themselves in these conversations and consider how we might increase digital literacy opportunities in all of our programs.

How other sectors benefit from arts education

Arts education promotes empathy, interpersonal understanding, social/emotional intelligence, teamwork, and creative problem-solving – all skills that can help students understand and generate solutions to the big issues facing us today.[26] The assets an arts program has to offer may be difficult to recognize within the university system for several reasons. Formalized arts programs reframe traditional academic practices with embodied learning, studio-based classrooms, and project-based assessment strategies, making them suspect as subjects for legitimate intellectual inquiry (for some). Initially, the study of art was limited to specialized schools and/or apprentice work. Only in the recent history of the academy have we seen the emergence of departments like dance, visual art, and theatre. Arts programs suffer from the belief that such a course of study is frivolous and can only lead to unemployment and poverty. Research refutes these myths as the skills arts students acquire are attractive to employers in many fields.

Because of the accelerated evolution of technology, the need for an adaptable education will continue to grow. Arts education, particularly the study of theatre, offers a comprehensive array of skills that can enhance and amplify the effectiveness and adaptability of many other fields of study. Storytelling has been a part of the human experience for nearly as long as recorded history.[27] Theatre training teaches students about the politics, history, and social concerns of a play – requiring them to understand events in context. Dramaturgy and text analysis promote critical thinking, ethics, and thematic conceptualization. Translating these ideas into design for a live production increases a student's understanding of aesthetics, architecture, and structural safety. Learning to play the story on a stage develops confidence in front of an audience, psychological and interpersonal understanding, and the ability to improvise. All areas of theatre enhance creative problem-solving and working in teams.[28] Arts education and theatre education, in particular, offer significant value for every student. Should such training become an integral component of an undergraduate degree across majors, theatre educators could be instrumental in helping all students on campus better position themselves for employment upon graduation.

The threat to theatre departments

Theatre departments are currently facing numerous existential threats. As administrators across the country struggle to balance their budgets, one of the easiest solutions is to cut programs that seem obsolete. A theatre program is a soft target as it carries with it a stigma of fun.[29] Learning can be enjoyable, but pleasure does not easily equate to serious study. Fun is not our only reputational challenge. We may be cut because we have failed to demonstrate value within the performance indicators of a neoliberal paradigm.[30] Enrollment is one of these indicators. Enrollment is declining for most institutions of higher education in the United States as a byproduct of shifting demographics. Enrollment equates to tuition revenue. Tuition revenue is weighed against program costs. A theatre department is expensive. A reduction in the number of enrolled theatre majors therefore becomes a direct threat to the longevity of a theatre program. Finding ways to increase the number of majors and/or the number of students taking theatre classes is critically important. Demonstrating the multidisciplinary application of our coursework to attract students from other fields is one way to make that happen.

Employability is another performance indicator. It is nearly impossible for a theatre department to demonstrate full-time employment in the field within 2–5 years following the completion of the degree. Some graduates may find theatre jobs here and there, but sustainable employment in the theatre for a significant number of majors so soon after graduation is simply not possible. This is partly because there are so few jobs in the theatre industry that offer full-time employment and so many students graduating with a theatre degree. Job placement statistics favor majors like engineering, nursing, and business where one can find a more favorable balance between employment opportunities and the number of graduates. Such grim placement statistics threaten theatre programs. To promise a theatre graduate strong opportunities for employment in the field shortly after graduation is dishonest and, according to Freeman, could one day land us in court for misrepresentation.[31] We cannot win the employment argument unless we demonstrate employment value in another way. "Art for art's sake" will not persuade. But providing evidence that the skills acquired with a theatre degree will make a student in any field more rather than less employable over the lifetime of a career is a strong defense.

One of a theatre department's greatest challenges is habit and tradition. Our departments were founded on an industry very different from the post-pandemic crisis we encounter today. The curriculum offered to students is generally structured – both in content and in form – to comply with the needs of the professional theatre industry. Unfortunately, the industry toward which we often direct our studies is the regional theatre movement of the 1970s, 1980s, and 1990s. Some departments have recognized the importance of radio, television, and film work and have included classes in those subjects on their roster. This is important for the minority of graduates who will find work in those industries. The theatre graduates in my study indicated that only 31% of them went on to establish careers as working artists in the theatre industry, and the majority of those respondents were early in their careers suggesting the possibility that some of them may choose to shift out of the theatre at a future point. How do we serve the other 69% of those who major in our programs and end up working in other fields? Theatre departments must think carefully about how to position their value to the institution at large, and how to market their ability to train students outside of the discipline of theatre as a contribution to the employability of the larger student body. This is not to say that theatre instructors should stop teaching the skills required to become a theatre artist. But if we do not find ways to expand our impact and demonstrate our value to other constituencies, our departments will continue to disappear.[32]

One of the advantages of an adaptive and more inclusive curriculum could be a shift in messaging to our students – those who choose to major and those who do not. We certainly want to offer training that allows those who have theatrical gifts to thrive in the theatre industry. But the reality is that most of our students will not have exceptional gifts, they will just be ordinarily talented and highly enthusiastic members of our student body. Even those with exceptional natural ability have no guarantee of success and may choose to leave the theatre industry at some point in their career. For some students, this inability to "make it in the business" can be internalized and interpreted as failure. That means that the majority of a graduating class may at some point perceive their decision to pursue theatre training as a mistake. Unless we change the conversation. This study has demonstrated that a theatre degree is a ticket to gainful employment in any number of fields. That is a win, not a loss. It is important to shift our message and make clear that, should a theatre graduate choose to change careers either right now or in the future, their degree will provide an important part of the training they need. Amplifying the message that theatre training is good for all professions is also good for our theatre students, and we serve them by making this clear throughout their course of study. Shifting the message to "theatre is not just for future stars but for all," could attract a larger population of non-majors to our classes. We need those students to help save our programs and they need us to help make them more employable.

Our training focus must shift

Theatre educators are currently training far too many aspiring theatre artists for an oversaturated job market. Hundreds (thousands?) of theatre students graduate each year equipped to join the artistic community, only to discover that it is nearly impossible for them to find work as theatre artists. There is work available, work in a variety of industries, but they may enter the job market unaware of this possibility or uninterested in working in another field. Focusing theatre education on training future theatre artists has an understandable precedent, one to which we have been doggedly attached despite the knowledge that most of our students are not finding work in the theatre. Peter Zazzali identified that there were over 150 theatre programs in the United States offering BFA and MFA degrees in 2015, and this did not include the hundreds of programs across the country offering a BA in theatre.[33] The expansion of these programs has created a glut of graduates who cannot possibly be employed within the limited number of jobs available in the professional theatre industry. Our educational focus must shift. We need to consider how to help our students broaden their professional aspirations to include the possibility of employment in other disciplines.

Although a BFA in theatre may be appropriate for a handful of exceptionally talented students who have the ability and the temperament to craft a full-time career in the theatre, there are simply too many programs training too many hopeful undergraduates for work they may never find. In contrast, a BA in theatre is designed to include at least some training in all areas of the discipline. This generalist training, rich with transferable skills, is a strong match with what the job market is currently seeking. The education offered by a BA in theatre mitigates the educator's ethical dilemma as this degree contributes directly to a student's employability in many fields. Rather than delaying the disappointment of a "failed" theatre career post-graduation for the majority of theatre graduates, we can prepare them to succeed, excel, and perhaps even out-compete some of their colleagues by explicating the interdisciplinary value of their degree during their college instruction. We would do well to reduce the number of BFA students, increase the number of BA students, and embed within both populations clear information regarding how their theatre degree can help them find work in many fields. In addition, we can begin expanding our curricular offerings and tailor them to include students in other disciplines, thereby increasing our enrollment numbers and demonstrating campus-wide value.

Recommendations for change

To save our programs and shift the message about our value, we need to find ways to adapt to the current economic realities facing many institutions. This will require us to defy tradition, consider new paradigms, and map our action plans in partnership with those who oversee our departments. Most administrators will welcome information that makes the advocacy for theatre departments easier. Some may be skeptical about the value of a theatre degree and may require persuasion. If so, then it is our job to position a compelling argument. There are multiple strategies we can employ. Let me offer a few suggestions.

1 *Find ways to integrate theatre training into non-theatre disciplines.*

   I have worked with a physicist at Cornell to develop workshops that teach scientists to use improvisation exercises to improve their public speaking skills.[34] Teaching public speaking to the non-theatre student body is an obvious mode of engagement, and I am hopeful that many theatre departments already offer this opportunity. But what about also offering role-playing exercises for leadership skills in the business school? Or Wicked Problem classes for engineering students?[35] Or creativity exercises for pre-med students? The Cornell Vet School produces a musical every year. I expect this is an enjoyable endeavor, but a theatre specialist could help those students recognize how what they are learning through theatre practice is interdisciplinary. There are many possibilities in this category. They all require leaving the comfort of the department and engaging with students in other disciplines in other locations on campus, many of whom may need to be persuaded about the value of creative activities. Such efforts would increase the visibility and impact of what we do and begin to change the message around theatre training.

2 *Tailor-make theatre classes for non-theatre departments.*

In this instance, theatre educators invite students (or possibly faculty) to come to the spaces located within the theatre department. This dislocation alone can be an important learning moment as the architecture in most theatre classrooms differs from the standard lecture hall. What I propose here is not a designated section of a class for non-majors that is already on offer, although that is also helpful. Rather, this is a class created via a consultative process with another department that addresses a specific need in their student body. Consider an anthropology class that offers off-campus fieldwork requiring students to engage with populations different from their own (Indigenous communities, rural farmers, and addiction survivors, as some examples). To prepare for this learning experience, students would need to develop high-level interpersonal communication skills. The theatre department could offer such a class in a drama classroom, and tailor the exercises to train these students to succeed in that work. Identifying such specific needs and then finding the time and resources to create these classes would be challenging, but imagine the educational impact such a class could offer.

3 *Construct project-based classes that intentionally mix disciplines.*

In this scenario, we bring together students from engineering, art & design, philosophy, and biology and task them with a semester-long problem-based project. Perhaps they have been asked to save a rare ecosystem that is disappearing due to climate change. A theatre instructor, co-instructing with professors from other disciplines, could oversee the development of this project, guiding students toward an end-of-term public presentation of their results for an invited audience. This interdisciplinary problem-based approach is an important new direction for higher education. The Stanford 2025 initiative created educational collaborations based on this idea. They determined quickly in the process of constructing and implementing their educational initiatives that the most successful courses were those that brought together disparate disciplines. This experiment resulted in several new degree programs, including Artificial Intelligence for Social Inquiry, Quantitative Global Affairs, and Right Brain Finance.[36]

4 *Encourage double majors at your university.*

Some of the study participants identified either appreciating their double major or recommending such a course to others. A double major that includes theatre study allows students to amplify their qualifications in many fields and can do much to calm worried parents. To keep costs reasonable, administrators may have to adjust requirements for graduation as not all students can afford five to six years of college study.

5 *Engage with alumni.*

Many departments that have famous alumni in theatre and film are quick to invite them to campus to speak with students. This offers both knowledge and pleasure to theatre majors. But what about those alumni who have flourishing and important careers in other fields? They constitute the majority of graduates, and they present an ideal opportunity to demonstrate the variety of career pathways available to a theatre major. These graduates know best how to advise students who might wish to position themselves for success in another field.

6 *Talk with administrators.*

I recognize and acknowledge that, given the sacredness of hierarchy in the academy, opportunities for faculty members to speak directly to the dean or the provost may not be possible. Chairs are well positioned for this conversation, but they may need support and resources to structure their argument. Whatever the politics required to engage in dialogue, find a way to help administrators see the value a theatre department offers to the entire institution. This will help protect theatre programs and may even position a department for unexpected sources of revenue that could be used to start some interdisciplinary initiatives.

7 *Talk with your students.*

Graduates of theatre programs are one of the greatest sources of advertising for the value of a theatre degree. Find ways to be explicit about the transferable skills of theatre training while you are teaching them. Give them the language to share with others about the amazing education a theatre degree can offer and plant seeds regarding how a theatre degree is useful in a variety of fields. If we only talk to theatre students about the theatre industry, they may miss that they are learning a whole collection of skills that have been identified as critically important to employment in a range of fields.

8 *Collaborate with the career counselors on campus.*

It is a career counselor's job to help students find an appropriate pathway to employment upon graduation. Do the career counselors on your campus understand the potential impact of a theatre degree on future employability? Could your department help support their efforts by offering career preparation workshops in a variety of transferable skills? This could be an exciting way to expand the reach of the department, increase visibility for the courses your department offers, and help shape the message about the value of theatre training.

What the graduates in this study told us

Each chapter in this book has included extensive research on current educational and economic trends and a reality check by the 1,132 participants in the survey. Here is an overview of what we learned from them.

Chapter 1: Passion versus practicality

Half of the survey participants were in an early career stage. Most graduates chose to major in theatre initially because of the love of the field (30%), while the more practical believed a degree would help them prepare for a career in the theatre (21%). Participants overwhelmingly indicated they had planned for a professional career in the theatre when choosing to major (79%). From this information, we learned that actual talent in the field did not drive many students toward a theatre major. Rather, students (most likely) intended to pursue a career in the theatre and had various motivations for doing so.

Chapter 2: Patterns of employment

Based on an adaptation of the Creative Trident methodology,[37] the study asked participants to identify their employment according to the following categories: Working Artist, Blended-Career, Shifted Career-Creative Skills, and Shifted Career-Has Left the Field. These four categories captured the diversity of employment patterns for theatre graduates and accommodated the variety of career types experienced by participants.

Blended-Career received the greatest number of affiliations (41%), followed by Working Artist (31%), Shifted-Creative (20%), Shifted-Left (7%), and Other (1%). Here we learned that almost 70% of theatre graduates will work partially or entirely outside the field of theatre at some point in their career. Factors such as geographic location and institution size had minimal impact on these numbers. When examining income levels, we learned that a) most graduates (51%) earned between $30,000 and $75,000 annually, and those who earned more than $100,000 per year most often identified as Shifted-Creatives.

Participants shared some details about their non-arts employment, indicating education as a strong alternative pathway for those with a Blended-Career. Those who shifted careers (Shifted-Creative / Shifted-Left) chose Other as their non-arts category and then offered an astonishing array of fields in which they were working. The reasons for shifting away from theatre as their primary form of employment included needing more stability (25% / 25%), wanting to make more money (18% / 19%), interest in another field (16% / 14%), and lack of opportunity (14% / 18%). From this information we learned that the majority of participants constructed blended careers or shifted out of the theatre industry at some point in their career; these graduates found employment in a wide variety of fields; the majority made a moderate income; and their reasons for leaving were variable and driven by individual circumstance.

Chapter 3: Skills for all professions

When asked whether a theatre degree contributed to participants' current employment, the majority of participants answered with *To a great extent* (65%). When asked which transferable skills were acquired with the degree, the top three answers were *collaboration* (90%), *working within a team* (87%), and *creativity* (83%).

When asked which skills they were applying to their current employment, all of the 16 skills on the list received high marks on utility with *interpersonal communication* (75%), *professionalism* (72%), and *adaptive problem-solving* (72%) receiving the three highest scores in *Almost Constantly*. When examining skills used in current employment by trident category, two skills were prevalent across employment types: *interpersonal communication* and *adaptive problem-solving.*

Chapter 4: Value versus expense

A college education is expensive, and the cost continues to grow. To better understand how participants perceived the value of their degree, the study asked if they were satisfied with the education they had received. The majority indicated at least moderate satisfaction with 87%. Given their current employment circumstances, would graduates major in theatre again? 89% responded yes. Did they believe the degree to be worth the money spent? 84% answered yes to this question. From this information we learned that most participants were satisfied with their degree, they would major in theatre again if given the chance, and they believed the degree to have been worth the money spent.

In summary

This book offers evidence of the employment value of a theatre degree and the skills that comprise it. To save our theatre programs from becoming the victims of budget reductions, we must work together to change the message regarding how a theatre education contributes to a student's employability. I have offered data to support the process of message-changing, and I hope that others in my field will join me in this journey. Motivating theatre departments to expand their approach to theatre training and become more discipline-inclusive is critically important and time-sensitive as more and more theatre programs are removed from the curriculum to help administrators balance budgets. Two important results from this study are simultaneously true: (1) most theatre graduates will not construct a full-time career in the theatre. This could be misunderstood by politicians, administrators, and the general public to mean that a degree in theatre delivers limited employment value. (2) Every college student could benefit from the skills offered by theatre training as those skills are precisely what employers are seeking.

All students would have an opportunity to benefit from theatre training if more members of the educational community were aware of its value, and if theatre educators were willing to adapt their curriculum to accommodate them. Theatre graduates who have shifted to other fields and applied the skills learned with their theatre education can testify to the interdisciplinarity and wide-ranging professional applicability of a theatre degree. To save theatre programs and to protect the skills training important to college students in every discipline, we must work together to persuade the administration and the general public that cutting arts programs like theatre will hurt not help higher education.

I hope that the information contained in this book will be helpful to all who have an interest in theatre study – those who aspire to work in the field, those charged with teaching them, and those who engage in the struggle to save theatre programs across the country. Theatre education is critically important, not just for aspiring theatre artists, but for every student seeking to arm themselves for a dynamic and adaptable career in any field.

Notes

1 Palfreyman, D., & Temple, P. (2017). *Universities and colleges: A very short introduction* (Vol. 545). Oxford University Press.
2 Comunian, R., Faggian, A., & Jewell, S. (2011). Winning and losing in the creative industries: An analysis of creative graduates' career opportunities across creative disciplines. *Cultural Trends, 20*(3–4), 291–308.
3 Rancourt, D. E. (2020, November 20). *Graduates need to prioritize versatility when entering the workforce.* University Affairs. https://universityaffairs.ca/career-advice/career-advice-article/graduates-need-to-prioritize-versatility-when-entering-the-workforce/
4 Bok, D. (2020). *Higher expectations: Can colleges teach students what they need to know in the 21st Century?* Princeton University Press.
5 Haukka, S. (2011). Education-to-work transitions of aspiring creatives. *Cultural Trends, 20*(1), 41–64.
6 Palfreyman, D., & Temple, P. (2017). *Universities and colleges: A very short introduction* (Vol. 545). Oxford University Press.
7 Cevallos, F.J. (2012). Against the windmills: The commoditization of higher education In M. Fennell & S. D. Miller (Eds.), *Presidential perspectives: A higher education presidential thought leadership series* (pp. 9–18). Association of International Education Administrators.
8 Freeman, J. (2012). Drama at a time of crisis: Actor training, performance study and the creative workplace. *International Journal of Education & the Arts, 13*(4), 1–22.
9 Bancino, R., & Zevalkink, C. (2007). Soft skills: The new curriculum for hard-core technical professionals. *Techniques: Connecting Education and Careers (J1), 82*(5), 20–22.
10 Cox, J. (2020, July 2). *Move over STEM: Why SHAPE skills will add true value to tomorrow's workforce.* Forbes. https://www.forbes.com/sites/josiecox/2020/07/02/stem-skills-education-value-future-of-work-shape/?sh=10f6470a370a
11 Bazalgette, P. (2020, June 21). *Why the arts must shape our future.* The Guardian. https://www.theguardian.com/commentisfree/2020/jun/21/why-the-arts-must-shape-our-future
12 Chronicle of Higher Education (Producer). (2020). *What employers want: An exclusive survey from The Chronicle of Higher Education* [webinar]. https://www.chronicle.com/page/what-employers-want?cid2=gen_login_refresh&cid=gen_sign_in
13 Lindemann, D. J., & Tepper, S. J. (2012). *Painting with broader strokes: Reassessing the value of an arts degree–based on the results of the 2010 Strategic National Arts Alumni Project. Special Report 1.* Strategic National Arts Alumni Project.
14 Matthews, N. (2011). Transition or translation? Thinking through media and cultural studies students' experiences after graduation. *Cultural Studies Review, 17*(2), 28–48.

15 Ferguson, B. (2018, May 12). *Don't apologize for your liberal arts degree*. The Globe and Mail Inc. https://www.theglobeandmail.com/news/national/education/dont-apologize-for-your-liberal-arts-degree/article17684918/
16 Freeman, J. (2012). Drama at a time of crisis: Actor training, performance study and the creative workplace. *International Journal of Education & the Arts, 13*(4), 1–22.
17 Reddick, R. (2022). *Campus skills report*. Coursera, Inc. https://www.coursera.org/skills-reports/campus
18 Essig, L. (2009). Suffusing entrepreneurship education throughout the theatre curriculum. *Theatre Topics, 19*(2), 117–124.
19 Stokes, P. J. (2017). *Higher education and employability: New models for integrating study and work*. Harvard Education Press.
20 Blumenstyk, G. (2019). *Career-ready education: Beyond the skills gap, tools and tactics for an evolving economy.* Chronicle of Higher Education.
21 Kivunja, C. (2014). Theoretical perspectives of how digital natives learn. *International Journal of Higher Education, 3*(1), 94–109.
22 Kivunja, C. (2014). Theoretical perspectives of how digital natives learn. *International Journal of Higher Education, 3*(1), 94–109.
23 Van Laar, E., Van Deursen, A. J., Van Dijk, J. A., & De Haan, J. (2017). The relation between 21st-century skills and digital skills: A systematic literature review. *Computers in Human Behavior, 72*, 577–588.
24 Van Laar, E., Van Deursen, A. J., Van Dijk, J. A., & De Haan, J. (2017). The relation between 21st-century skills and digital skills: A systematic literature review. *Computers in Human Behavior, 72*, 577–588.
25 Adedoyin, O. B., & Soykan, E. (2023). Covid-19 pandemic and online learning: The challenges and opportunities. *Interactive Learning Environments, 31*(2), 863–875.
26 Hawkins, J. (2015). Countering critique: Expressing the value of the arts through the artistic rebuttal project. *The Journal of Arts Management, Law, and Society, 45*(2), 100–118.
27 Yılmaz, R., & Ciğerci, F. M. (2019). A brief history of storytelling: From primitive dance to digital narration. In R. Yilmaz & F.M. Ciğerci (Eds.), *Handbook of research on transmedia storytelling and narrative strategies* (pp. 1–14). IGI Global.
28 Kondoyianni, A., Lenakakis, A., & Tsiotsos, N. (2013). Intercultural and lifelong learning based on educational drama. *Scenario: A Journal of Performative Teaching, Learning, Research, 7*(2), 28–48.
29 Kindelan, N. (2012). *Artistic literacy: Theatre studies and a contemporary liberal education*. Springer.
30 Bowen, D., & Kisida, B. (2019). Investigating causal effects of arts education experiences: Experimental evidence from Houston's Arts Access Initiative. Rice University's Kinder Institute for Urban Research. *Research Brief for the Houston Independent School District, 7*(3).
31 Freeman, J. (2012). Drama at a time of crisis: Actor training, performance study and the creative workplace. *International Journal of Education & the Arts, 13*(4), 1–22.
32 Grassian, D. (2015). The new U: Higher education in the 21st century. *Journal of Higher Education Management 30*(1), 216–232.
33 Zazzali, P. (2016). *Acting in the academy: The history of professional actor training in US Higher Education.* Routledge.
34 Cohen, I., & Dreyer-Lude, M. (2020). *Finding your research voice: Story telling and theatre skills for bringing your presentation to life*. Springer Nature.
35 Buchanan, R. (1992). Wicked problems in design thinking. *Design Issues, 8*(2), 5–21.
36 For more information on these innovations look under "Unexpected Intersections" at this link: http://www.stanford2025.com/axis-flip
37 Higgs, P., Cunningham, S., & Pagan, J. (2007) *Australia's creative economy: Definitions of the segments and sectors.* ARC Centre of Excellence for Creative Industries & Innovation (CCI).

Methodology

Introduction

In a time of economic precarity and institutional crisis, arts programs in higher education are under threat. Although research has demonstrated that arts education contributes to the economy[1] and that arts graduates are generally satisfied with their degrees,[2] administrators lack statistical evidence to support their advocacy for programs like theatre. This study helps fill that gap by offering detailed, disaggregated data that maps where theatre graduates have been working, which skills they have applied to that work, and the level of satisfaction they have experienced with their theatre education.

This investigation focused on three research questions:

1 Where do graduates of four-year undergraduate theatre programs in the United States find work, and what is the pattern of that work over time and at any one time?
2 Which skills acquired with this theatre degree have been applied to employment?
3 How satisfied are graduates of these theatre programs with the employment value of their theatre degree?

Research framework

Research questions 1 (where do graduates find work and what does that work look like) and 3 (satisfaction of degree, given current employment) utilized a modified version of Higgs, Cunningham, and Pagan's Creative Trident Framework.[3] The Modified Creative Trident (Figure 6.1) allowed for the disaggregation of theatre employment and exposed the complexity of the employment patterns of theatre graduates.

In this modified trident, theatre employment patterns fell into four distinct categories, determining which graduates were working inside or outside of the field and whether they were applying their theatre skills to their current employment. Research question 2 (skills acquired and then applied to employment) engaged an adapted 21st-century skills paradigm to include

		Creative and Cultural Sector	
		Yes	No
Utilization of Creative Skills for Employment	Yes	**Working Artists** *(working full time in the theatre industry)*	**Shifted Career Creative Skills** *(working outside of the theatre industry applying theatre skills)*
	No	**Blended Career** *(working inside and outside of the theatre industry)*	**Shifted Career Has Left the Field** *(working full time outside of the theatre industry)*

Figure 6.1 Modified Creative Trident

a compilation of skills recommended by scholars and currently sought by employers.[4] This final list of skills was created using a combination of professional experience in theatre education and theatre practice, archival data acquired in an exploratory survey conducted in the Fall of 2018, and an aggregate of the most common skills identified in the research on 21st-century skills. The final list included 16 skills: *adaptive problem-solving, collaboration, conflict management, creativity, critical thinking, cultural sensitivity, empathy, interpersonal communication, leadership, persuasion, professionalism, public speaking, self-direction, technology, time management*, and *working within a team* (Figure 6.1).

Research design

This was a cross-sectional study focused on Bachelor of Arts (BA) and/or Bachelor of Fine Arts (BFA) graduates of undergraduate theatre programs in four-year universities in the United States. The study utilized a convergent parallel mixed-methods approach[5] with a concurrent nested design[6] to gather quantitative and qualitative data about employment circumstances, skills application, and levels of satisfaction with a theatre degree. A mixed-methods design allowed a comparison of quantitative and qualitative data to contextualize the findings, providing an opportunity for the integration and analysis of statistical employment data against the perceived value of the degree.

Sampling strategy

The study used a non-probability strategy to gather participants through a combination of convenience and snowball sampling. An original attempt to utilize alumni databases from universities across the United States was unsuccessful due to poor data collection by individual departments and/or lack of access to alumni records. Instead, the study engaged a combination of Facebook posts to public and private networks and direct, personalized emails to chairs and colleagues across the country. All who received the call for participants were encouraged to expand the reach of the study by sharing the survey with their networks. This two-pronged strategy resulted in a total of 1,391 responses to the survey.

Data collection

Before gathering data, this study was approved by the Institutional Research Board in the Office of Research and Development at the University of Missouri in compliance with research ethics and standards. Quantitative data captured participants' employment category (as mapped in the Modified Creative Trident), the specific fields in which they were working, and the skills they were using in their employment, as well as other employment-related data and demographic information. Qualitative questions (including Other for several quantitative questions) provided space for participants to share additional information not otherwise indicated in the survey. One open-ended question at the end of the survey allowed participants to share anything else they found important to communicate. Data was collected during January and February of 2020 using an online Qualtrics survey consisting of 19 questions (15 quantitative and 4 qualitative), plus a qualifying question at the top of the survey.

The survey contained the following questions:

Qualifying question

Did you graduate with a four-year degree in Theatre Arts in the United States? (any specialization)

- Yes (required to continue with the survey)
- No (participant not allowed to take the survey)

Demographic data (1, 2, 16, 17, 18)

1 What year did you graduate with a degree in theatre? (*quantitative*)
2 How would you categorize your institution? (*quantitative*)

  a Small private university. (0–2,500 students)
  b Medium-sized private university. (2,501–10,000 students)
  c Large private university. (>10,000 students)
  d Small public university. (0–2,500 students)
  e Medium-sized public university. (2,501–10,000 students)

- f Large public university. (>10,000 students)
- g Ivy League institution. (Brown, Columbia, Cornell, Dartmouth, Harvard, University of Pennsylvania, Princeton, Yale)

16 Where are you currently located? (*quantitative*)

- a Northeast (ME, NH, VT, MA, RI, CT, NY, NJ, DE, PA, MD)
- b Southeast (VA, WV, GA, FL, NC, SC, AL, LA, MS, KY, TN, AR)
- c Midwest (OH, MI, WI, IL, MN, IN, MO, IA, ND, SD, NE, KS, OK, TX)
- d West (WA, CA, OR, MT, ID, NM, CO, WY, UT, NV, AZ, HI, AK)
- e U.S. territory
- f International
- g Other (please specify) [*qualitative*]

17 What is your gender? (*quantitative*)

- a Female
- b Male
- c Non-binary/third gender
- d Prefer to self-describe
- e Prefer not to say

18 What is your current level of income? (*quantitative*)

- a $0–$15,000
- b $15,001–$30,000
- c $30,001–$50,000
- d $50,001–$75,000
- e $75,001–$100,000
- f >$100,001
- g Prefer not to say

Research question one (4, 5, 6, 8, 13): Where were graduates working?

4 Did you plan to work professionally in the theatre when you chose to major in theatre? (*quantitative*)

- a Yes.
- b No.
- c. Maybe.

5 In what areas of theatre were you primarily interested? (choose all that apply) (*quantitative*)

- a Acting.
- b Design.
- c Stage Management.

- d Technical Production.
- e Construction (sets, lights, costumes).
- f Marketing.
- g Producing.
- h Other (please specify). [*qualitative*]

6 How would you categorize your current professional relationship to theatre practice? (choose one) (*quantitative*)

- a **Working artist** (making a living in the theatre industry).
  - 1 You currently work in:
    - 1 Theatre.
    - 2 Film/TV.
    - 3 Trade Shows.
    - 4 Cruise Ships.
    - 5 Other (please specify). [*qualitative*]
  - 2 You are employed as:
    - 1 Performer.
    - 2 Designer.
    - 3 Technician.
    - 4 Front of House Staff.
    - 5 Marketing Staff.
    - 6 Producer.

7 Other (please specify). [*qualitative*]

- b **Blended-career** (working in another field while still practicing theatre).
  - 1 What percentage of your work hours do you spend working in theatre?
    - 1 0–25%
    - 2 26–50%
    - 3 51–75%
    - 4 More than 75%
  - 2 What percentage of your work hours do you spend working in another field?
    - 1 0–25%
    - 2 26–50%
    - 3 51–75%
    - 4 More than 75%
  - 3 Generally speaking, what is the other field in which you work?
    - 1 Education or training.
    - 2 Business.

3 Hospitality or food service.
4 Marketing or advertising.
5 IT or computer service.
6 Care-taking (child or elderly care, for example).
7 Travel or tourism.
8 Sales.
9 Other (please specify). [*qualitative*]

c Shifted career with applied creative skills (in another field).

1 Generally speaking, what is the other field in which you work? (choose all that currently apply)

1 Education or training.
2 Business.
3 Hospitality or food service.
4 Marketing or advertising.
5 IT or computer service.
6 Care-taking (child or elderly care, for example).
7 Travel or tourism.
8 Sales.
9 Other (please specify). [*qualitative*]

2 Why did you shift your field of employment? (choose all that currently apply)

1 Lack of opportunities in the theatre.
2 Developed an interest in another field.
3 Wanted to make more money.
4 Needed more stability in my career.
5 Other (please specify). [*qualitative*]

d **Shifted career** (has left the field).

1 Generally speaking, what is the field in which you work? (choose all that currently apply)

1 Education or training.
2 Business.
3 Hospitality or food service.
4 Marketing or advertising.
5 IT or computer service.
6 Care-taking (child or elderly care, for example).
7 Travel or tourism.
8 Sales.
9 Other (please specify). [*qualitative*]

2 Why did you shift your field of employment? (choose all that currently apply)

1 Lack of opportunities in the theatre.
2 Developed an interest in another field.
3 Wanted to make more money.
4 Needed more stability in my career.
5 Other (please specify). [*qualitative*]

8 When asked to describe your profession to other people, what do you say? (artist, graphic designer, entrepreneur, etc.) (*qualitative*)

13 Since graduation with your theatre degree, have you experienced periods of unemployment? (*quantitative*)

a No.
b Yes.

How long were you unemployed?

- Less than six months.
- Six months to one year.
- One to two years.
- More than two years.

Research question two (10, 11, 12): Which skills were graduates using?

10 Please indicate which skills you use in your current employment and to what degree. (Select all that apply.) (*quantitative*)

Table 6.1 Skills used in current employment

Adaptive problem solving	Not at All ○	A Little ○	Sometimes ○	Often ○	Almost Constantly ○
Collaboration	Not at All ○	A Little ○	Sometimes ○	Often ○	Almost Constantly ○
Conflict management	Not at All ○	A Little ○	Sometimes ○	Often ○	Almost Constantly ○
Creativity	Not at All ○	A Little ○	Sometimes ○	Often ○	Almost Constantly ○
Critical thinking	Not at All ○	A Little ○	Sometimes ○	Often ○	Almost Constantly ○

Cultural sensitivity	Not at All ○	A Little ○	Sometimes ○	Often ○	Almost Constantly ○
Empathy	Not at All ○	A Little ○	Sometimes ○	Often ○	Almost Constantly ○
Interpersonal communication	Not at All ○	A Little ○	Sometimes ○	Often ○	Almost Constantly ○
Leadership	Not at All ○	A Little ○	Sometimes ○	Often ○	Almost Constantly ○
Persuasion	Not at All ○	A Little ○	Sometimes ○	Often ○	Almost Constantly ○
Professionalism	Not at All ○	A Little ○	Sometimes ○	Often ○	Almost Constantly ○
Public speaking	Not at All ○	A Little ○	Sometimes ○	Often ○	Almost Constantly ○
Self-direction	Not at All ○	A Little ○	Sometimes ○	Often ○	Almost Constantly ○
Technology	Not at All ○	A Little ○	Sometimes ○	Often ○	Almost Constantly ○
Time-management	Not at All ○	A Little ○	Sometimes ○	Often ○	Almost Constantly ○
Working within a team	Not at All ○	A Little ○	Sometimes ○	Often ○	Almost Constantly ○
Other: (please specify) [*qualitative*]	Not at All ○	A Little ○	Sometimes ○	Often ○	Almost Constantly ○

11 Please indicate which of the following skills you acquired with your theatre degree. (Select all that apply.) (*quantitative*)

Table 6.2 Skills acquired with the theatre degree

Adaptive problem solving	○
Collaboration	○
Conflict management	○
Creativity	○
Critical thinking	○
Cultural sensitivity	○

Empathy	○
Interpersonal communication	○
Leadership	○
Persuasion	○
Professionalism	○
Public speaking	○
Self-direction	○
Technology	○
Time-management	○
Working within a team	○
Other: (please specify) [*qualitative*]	○

12 To what extent has your degree in theatre contributed to your current employment? (*quantitative*)

- a To a great extent.
- b To some extent.
- c To a small extent.
- d Not at all.

Research question three (3, 7, 9, 14, 15): What is the level of satisfaction with the degree?

3 How or why did you decide to major in theatre? (*qualitative*)

7 How would you describe your level of satisfaction with your employment situation? (*quantitative*)

- a Very satisfied.
- b Moderately satisfied.
- c Moderately unsatisfied.
- d Very unsatisfied.

9 Please describe your current theatre practice? (freelance director, community theatre designer, board member, etc.) (*qualitative*)

14 If you had it to do all over again, would you choose to major in theatre? (*quantitative*)

- a Definitely yes.
- b Maybe yes.
- c Maybe no.
- d Definitely no.

15 Do you believe that a theatre degree is a worthy investment of tuition dollars? (*quantitative*)

- a Definitely yes.
- b Maybe yes.
- c Maybe no.
- d Definitely no.

Other information

19 Is there any information that you would like to share that was not captured by the questions on this survey? (*qualitative*)

Data analysis

Before beginning data analysis, the original pool of 1,391 participants was reduced to 1,132 by removing all participants who failed to complete the survey as well as those who answered "No" to having graduated with a BA or BFA degree in theatre in the United States but continued to answer questions in the survey. Quantitative data was analyzed within multiple comparative contexts using Microsoft Excel and Stata statistics software to extract descriptive statistics and determine relationships among the data variables. The study relied on the Modified Creative Trident and the 21st-century skills frameworks to establish validity. Qualitative data was analyzed using open coding to identify patterns, followed by axial coding to group these patterns into themes. The Framework Method[7] was applied to the final question in the survey to extract and interpret themes and patterns.

As the principal investigator graduated with an undergraduate degree in theatre from an institution in the United States, there was some concern regarding bias in the data collection and analysis. Having served as the chair of a theatre department that experienced budgetary pressures, there was a vested interest in the findings from this study. This also offered potential for bias. Using a Facebook network to initiate data collection presented a third opportunity for bias as the call for participants was posted to the general public as well as the professional and personal networks of the principal investigator. The personal networks of the principal investigator contained theatre graduates and theatre practitioners, some of whom were former students and colleagues. The snowball networking strategy worked to mitigate these concerns.

Limitations and assumptions

The sampling methods in the study represent one possible limitation. The choice to participate in the survey could have been influenced by personal perceptions of the participant's career to date. This could have resulted in a skew toward a more positive or a more negative view of the relationship between the theatre degree and current employment. Whether these limitations presented a threat to the validity of the data may be unknowable, but the process of soliciting participants for the study has exposed a need for easier access to reliable alumni information for studies of this nature.

The study assumed that an aggregate of survey responses would represent the typical experience of a theatre graduate from a university in the United States. Although the study participants' programs may not have contained a precise match in curriculum, the study assumed that participants had acquired theatre skills during their course of study similar to those listed by the National Association of Schools of Theatre (NAST).[8] The study assumed that participants applied their classroom education to a theatre production at some point during their studies and that this laboratory experience provided its own teaching environment. The study also assumed that differences in specialization (acting, directing, stage management, dramaturgy, etc.) were not an important influence on the data. Finally, the study assumed that participants shared a common understanding of all terms used in the survey as applied to a general Theatre Arts context.

Recommendations for future research

1 Case studies investigating the awareness and application of employable skills within a theatre context.
2 A review of the transferable skills deficit within various disciplines from a cross-section of departments on college campuses.
3 Case studies involving any of the recommendations provided in Chapter 5 to determine whether these suggestions contributed to increasing the perceived value of a theatre degree.
4 A replication of this study with a new population of theatre graduates to assess its validity.

Notes

1 Goldsmith, B., & Bridgstock, R. (2015). Embedded creative workers and creative work in education. *Journal of Education and Work, 28*(4), 369–387.
2 Lindemann, D. J., & Tepper, S. J. (2012). *Painting with broader strokes: Reassessing the value of an arts degree--based on the results of the 2010 Strategic National Arts Alumni Project. Special Report 1.* Strategic National Arts Alumni Project.
3 Higgs, P., Cunningham, S., & Pagan, J. (2007) *Australia's creative economy: Definitions of the segments and sectors.* ARC Centre of Excellence for Creative Industries & Innovation (CCI).
4 Blumenstyk, G. (2019). *Career-ready education: Beyond the skills gap, tools and tactics for an evolving economy.* Chronicle of Higher Education.
5 Creswell, J. W. (2014). *Research design: Qualitative, quantitative, and mixed methods approaches* (4th. ed.). Sage.
6 Creswell, J. W., Plano-Clark, V. L., Gutmann, M. L., & Hanson, W. E. (2003). Advanced mixed methods research designs. In A. Tashakkori & C. Teddlie (Eds.), *Handbook of mixed methods in social and behavioral research* (pp. 209–240). Sage.
7 Srivastava, P., & Hopwood, N. (2009). A practical iterative framework for qualitative data analysis. *International Journal of Qualitative Methods, 8*(1), 76–84.
8 https://nast.arts-accredit.org

Jobs listed by survey participants

Academia
Accountant
Adjunct professor
Administration
Advocacy
Alumnae engagement
Animal care
Art dealer
Art development
Arts administration
Arts marketing
Associate producer
Audience services
Audio visual specialist
Audition studio manager
Autobody repair
Banker
Billing
Bookkeeping
Bookstore
Brewer
Broadcasting
Business affairs for television
Business analysis
Business owner
Carpenter
Casting director
Circus
Clerical work
College advising
Communication and marketing
Community engagement educator
Community outreach
Computer work
Construction
Consulting
Cooking show host
Corporate audio visual
Corporate education
Corporate events
Librarian
Lighting design
Lighting system sales
Live event production
Lyft
Manufacturing
Marketing
Marketing assistant
Medicine
Membership coordinator
Middle school teacher
Ministry
Modeling
Museum administration
Museum educator
Music
Music teacher
Non-profit management
Nursing
Office assistant
Office manager
Office temp work
Opera administration
Operations manager
Parenting
Personal training
Philanthropy
Photographer
Piano teacher
Poet
Politics
Preschool teacher
Production assistant
Production manager
Professor
Project manager
Props master
Psychiatric case management
Public administration
Publicist

Counselor
Culture worker
Customer service
Dance
Dance teacher
Development
Digital marketer
Digital platform designer
Editing
Education
Electrician
Emergency medical services
Energy analyst
Engineering
Entrepreneur
Escape room design
Event lighting
Event management
Fabricator
Face painting
Facilities management
Farm co-op manager
Farming
Fashion
Federal government manager
Fiction writer
Film/TV
Finance
Fitness industry
Flying trapeze school
Freelance fine artist
Fundraising
Furniture building
Government
Grant writing
Graphic design
Hair stylist
Handyman
Healthcare
Healthcare administrator
High school teacher
House manager
House the homeless
Human resources
Insurance
Interior design
Intimacy choreographer
International trade
Journalism
Landscape architecture
Lawyer
Legal assistant
Public service
Publishing
Quality assurance analyst
Real estate
Receptionist
Recorded media
Reporter
Research
Restaurant manager
Restaurant work
Retail
Ride share driving
Sales manager
Screen printing
Secretary
Server
Service industry
Sewing
Sexton
Small business owner
Soap maker
Social justice philanthropy
Social media producer
Social work
Special ed paraprofessional
Special events, concerts
Speech language pathology
STEM educator
Supply chain manager
Tailor
Talent agent
Talent buyer
Talk show host
Teaching artist
Teaching assistant
Tech entrepreneur
Technical operations
Television production
Theatre manager
Theatre teacher
Themed entertainment
Training facilitator
Transportation
University administrator
Urban missionary
Video editor
Video game development
Visual arts
Website writer
Writer
Yoga instruction

Index

For Product Safety Concerns and Information please contact our EU
representative GPSR@taylorandfrancis.com
Taylor & Francis Verlag GmbH, Kaufingerstraße 24, 80331 München, Germany

www.ingramcontent.com/pod-product-compliance
Lightning Source LLC
LaVergne TN
LVHW010935110826
845149LV00013B/2616

* 9 7 8 1 0 3 2 8 5 8 3 3 3 *